STICK TIGHT

Books by Kevin Johnson

Early Teen Devotionals

Can I Be a Christian Without Being Weird?
Could Someone Wake Me Up Before I Drool on the Desk?
Does Anybody Know What Planet My Parents Are From?
So Who Says I Have to Act My Age?
Was That a Balloon or Did Your Head Just Pop?
Who Should I Listen To?
Why Can't My Life Be a Summer Vacation?
Why Is God Looking for Friends?

Early Teen Discipleship

Get God: Make Friends With the King of the Universe
Wise Up: Stand Clear of the Unsmartness of Sin
Cross Train: Blast Through the Bible From Front to Back
Pray Hard: Talk to God With Total Confidence
See Jesus: Peer Into the Life and Mind of Your Master
Stick Tight: Glue Yourself to Godly Friends

Books for Youth

Catch the Wave!
Find Your Fit[1]
Find Your Fit Discovery Workbook[1]
Find Your Fit Leader's Guide[1]
God's Will, God's Best[2]
Jesus Among Other Gods: Youth Edition[3]
Look Who's Toast Now!
What's With the Dudes at the Door?[4]
What's With the Mutant in the Microscope?[4]
What Do Ya Know?
Where Ya Gonna Go?

---

*To find out more about Kevin Johnson's books or speaking availability
visit his Web site: www.thewave.org*

[1]with Jane Kise   [2]with Josh McDowell   [3]with Ravi Zacharias   [4]with James White

Glue Yourself to Godly Friends

STICK TIGHT

Kevin Johnson

BETHANY HOUSE

MINNEAPOLIS, MINNESOTA

Published by Bethany House Publishers
A Ministry of Bethany Fellowship International
11400 Hampshire Avenue South
Bloomington, Minnesota 55438
www.bethanyhouse.com

Printed in the United States of America by
Bethany Press International, Bloomington, Minnesota 55438

Library of Congress Cataloging-in-Publication Data

Johnson, Kevin (Kevin Walter)
    Stick tight : glue yourself to godly friends / by Kevin Johnson.
        p.   cm. — (Early teen discipleship)
Features key Bible verses on removable, pocket-sized cards.
Summary: Twenty-five anecdotes depict real-life situations for teenagers and their frinds, followed by questions and relevant Bible verses.
    ISBN 0-7642-2434-4 (pbk.)
    1. Friendship—Religious aspects—Christianity—Juvenile literature.
2. Christian teenagers—Religious life—Juvenile
literature. [1. Friendship.   2.Christian life.   3. Bible—Study and teaching.]   I. Title.
    BV4647.F7   .J63   2001
    241'.6762—dc21   2001002498

To Pastor Peter and Kay Yang

for your kindness to

a young kid in Taiwan.

KEVIN JOHNSON is the bestselling author or co-author of more than twenty books for youth, including *Can I Be a Christian Without Being Weird?* and *Catch the Wave!* A full-time author and speaker, he served as senior editor for adult nonfiction at Bethany House Publishers and pastored a group of more than four hundred sixth through ninth graders at Elmbrook Church in metro Milwaukee. While his training includes an M.Div. from Fuller Theological Seminary and a B.A. in English and Print Journalism from the University of Wisconsin–River Falls, his current interests include cycling, guitar, and shortwave radio. Kevin and his wife, Lyn, live in Minnesota with their three children—Nate, Karin, and Elise.

Contents

Part 3: The Best Friends You Can Find

Part 4: When Good Friends Go Bad

Part 5: Your Ultimate Best Friend

How to Use This Book

Welcome to *Stick Tight*. This book is part of the EARLY TEEN DISCIPLE-SHIP series, better remembered by its clever initials, ETD. I wrote ETD as a follow-up to my series of bestselling devotionals—books like *Can I Be a Christian Without Being Weird?* and *Could Someone Wake Me Up Before I Drool on the Desk?* ETD has one aim: to help you take your next step in becoming wildly devoted to Jesus. If you're ready to work on a vital, heart-to-heart, sold-out relationship with God, this is your series.

The goal of *Stick Tight* is to help you glue yourself to godly friends—and to stick tight with God, your ultimate friend. *Stick Tight* prods you toward that goal through twenty-five Bible studies de-signed to make you think—okay, without *totally* breaking your brain. It will help you

- dig into Scripture on your own;
- feed on insights that you might not otherwise find;
- hit the heart issues that push you away from God or pull you closer to him.

You can pick your own pace—anything from a study a day to a study a week. But here's what you'll find in each study:

- Your first stop is BRAIN DRAIN—your spot at the beginning of each lesson to spout what you think.
- Then there's FLASHBACK—a bit of background so you better understand what's coming up.
- Don't skip over the BIBLE CHUNK—a hand-picked Bible passage to read.
- You get STUFF TO KNOW—questions to help you dig into what a passage means.
- There's INSIGHT—facts about the passage you might not figure out on your own.
- DA'SCOOP—definitions of weird words.
- And SIDELIGHT—other Bible verses that let you see the topic from a different angle.

The other big questions are, well . . .

- BIG QUESTIONS—your chance to apply what you have learned to your life.
- Each study wraps up with a DEEP THOT—a thought to chew on.

But that's not the end.

- There's STICKY STUFF—a Bible verse to jam into your brain juice.
- ACT ON IT—a way to do something with what you just learned.
- And DIG ON—another Bible passage to unearth if you want more.

And one more thing: There are cards in the back of the book for all the verses in STICKY STUFF, with a few bonus cards thrown in—since we'd already killed the tree.

If you've got a pencil and know how to use it, you're all set.

EXCEPT FOR ONE THING You can study *Stick Tight* on your own. But you can also work through this book with a friend or in a group. After every five studies there's a page called "Talk About It." Nope—you don't have to cover every question on the page. There are too many to answer, so pick the ones that matter most to you.

Whenever you do an ETD study with one friend or a bunch, keep in mind three goals—and three big questions to help you remember those goals. And nope—you don't have to actually ask those questions each time, because that would feel canned. But each time you meet you want to

- EMPATHIZE: *What's gone on since the last time you got together?* To "empathize" means to put yourself in someone else's shoes. Galatians 6:2 tells us to "carry each other's burdens" (NIV), or to "share each other's troubles and problems" (NLT). Whether you call them "highs and lows," "wows and pows," "uppers and downers," or "wins and wedgies," take time to celebrate and support each other by chatting through life's important happenings and offering simple, to-the-point prayers.
- ENCOURAGE: *Where are you at with Jesus?* Hebrews 3:13 says to "encourage one another daily. . . so that none of you may be hardened by sin's deceitfulness." Religious rules apart from a relationship with God are deadly. So instead be real: Are you

growing closer to or wandering away from the Lord you're learning to follow? Is anything tripping you up?

- EQUIP: *What one truth are you going to take away from today that will help you live closer to Jesus?* Second Timothy 3:16–17 promises that "All Scripture is inspired by God and is useful to teach us what is true and to make us realize what is wrong in our lives. It straightens us out and teaches us to do what is right. It is God's way of preparing us in every way, fully equipped for every good thing God wants us to do" (NLT). Don't leave your get-together without one point of truth that will make a difference in your life. It might not be the thought or verse that anyone else picks. But grab at least one truth—and hang on tight by letting it make a difference in your life.

Got it? Not only is *Stick Tight* a study to do on your own, but better yet, it can help you grow your faith with your friends. You can pick a leader—a youth or adult—or take turns picking questions and talking through them as your time allows. Just keep the three big goals in mind.

Now you're ready. You can do it. Grow ahead and turn the page and get started.

PART 1

GOD'S
TOP
TO-DO'S

(1.) Job Number One—And Two
(Love is a big deal)

While everyone else in school mopes around trying to score a few measly yearbook signatures to prove they have friends, you've gathered a mob the size of a Super Bowl celebration. Lunchroom supervisors entertain the crowds lined up waiting for your autograph. Even your principal wedges himself into the front of the line. He begs you to sign his yearbook—and he says to let him know if he can do anything else to accommodate your swarming fans.

BRAIN DRAIN What would you like the crowds at your school to do to prove your wild popularity?

FLASHBACK Some people cringe at the thought of a follower of Jesus ever having lots of friends. Non-Christians figure Christians are too weird to be well-liked, and Christians suspect a believer must have committed some radically unholy act to get close to non-Christian folks. It's true that Jesus didn't run around signing yearbooks. He didn't make it his goal to win popularity contests. But next to God, Jesus made people the most important part of his life.

BIBLE CHUNK Read Matthew 22:34–40

(34) Hearing that Jesus had silenced the Sadducees, the Pharisees got together. (35) One of them, an expert in the law, tested him with this ques-

tion: (36) "Teacher, which is the greatest commandment in the Law?"

(37) Jesus replied: " 'Love the Lord your God with all your heart and with all your soul and with all your mind.' (38) This is the first and greatest commandment. (39) And the second is like it: 'Love your neighbor as yourself.' (40) All the Law and the Prophets hang on these two commandments."

STUFF TO KNOW Why do the Pharisees quiz Jesus?
What do you think they want to accomplish (verses 34–35)?

INSIGHT In this Bible Chunk you spot two groups of religious leaders. The Pharisees sought to sway the crowds, while the Sadducees sought political power and influence among leaders. Both groups try to trick Jesus into saying something stupid, because both see Jesus as a threat to their own popularity.

What exactly does the Pharisee ask Jesus? Why ask that (verse 36)?

What does Jesus rank number one on God's list of things to do with your life? Better yet, what *two* things does he yank to the top (verses 37–38)?

INSIGHT Jesus knows those leaders are like some church folk. They look totally religious yet they massively miss the point of the faith they supposedly follow. They forget that the whole goal of Scripture—"the Law and the Prophets"—is to help you put God first and to love people as much as you love yourself.

So what's it mean that all the teachings of the Bible "hang on these two commandments" (verse 40)?

INSIGHT Jesus points out that you can't disconnect loving God and loving people—or vice versa. If you hate the person sitting next to you, then you don't really love God. If you hate God, then your ugliness always spills out on people. Do these two commandments, and you're doing all the rest.

BIG QUESTIONS Some people act like they can get along just fine without other people—like they don't want or need friends. Know anyone who fits that description? What are they like?

How important are friends to you? When have you tried to survive without people? How did that work?

Do you really think it's possible for a Christian to be tightly connected to people and God at the same time? Why or why not?

Okay, let's be blunt. This friendship thing isn't so simple. In your real world, how might friends get in the way of following God?

And how might following and obeying God get in the way of making human friends?

INSIGHT If you're honest with yourself, you know that people and God don't always want the same thing. What one says is good, for example, the other might call evil. But Jesus was able—somehow—to make *both* loving God and loving people workable and utterly important.

DEEP THOT God might not plan for you to be wildly popular, but you can be sure that he put relationships at the center of the universe he made—and that his plan is for you to stick tight with *both* him and the people he made. That's real friendship, God-style. And that's what God has put at the top of his to-do list for you.

STICKY STUFF Get a handle on God's top priorities by memorizing Matthew 22:37–39. There's a handy card in the back of the book to help you out.

ACT ON IT Talk with a mature Christian or two about how they have made *both* loving God and loving people big things in life. Ask the questions under "Big Questions."

DIG ON Check John 15:9–17 for another Bible Chunk where Jesus ties together loving God and loving people.

2. Locating True Love
(Where love comes from)

I'm in way over my head, Megan thinks as she and Nikki sit talking in the dark on the dock at Megan's cabin. "I've accepted the fact that my parents have split up for good," Nikki says. "They're still too busy fighting for either of them to really love me. But where has God been through all this? I've never felt his love!" As Nikki puts her head in her hands and cries, Megan wonders what to say.

BRAIN DRAIN How would you answer someone who says she's never felt loved?

FLASHBACK If you want to know what sticking tight is all about, you've got to check with John, the guy who wrote the fourth book of the New Testament as well as three skinny letters named after him toward the end of the Bible. John understood God's love, and in this Bible Chunk "the disciple whom Jesus loved" (John 21:20) explains the huge part love is to play in your life. He has an answer for everyone who isn't sure God's love is real.

BIBLE CHUNK Read 1 John 4:7–21

(7) Dear friends, let us love one another, for love comes from God. Everyone who loves has been born of God and knows God. (8) Whoever does not love does not know God, because God is love. (9) This is how God showed his love among us: He sent his one and only Son into the world that we might live through him. (10) This is love: not that we loved God, but that he loved us and sent his Son as an atoning sacrifice for our

sins. (11) Dear friends, since God so loved us, we also ought to love one another. (12) No one has ever seen God; but if we love one another, God lives in us and his love is made complete in us.

(13) We know that we live in him and he in us, because he has given us of his Spirit. (14) And we have seen and testify that the Father has sent his Son to be the Savior of the world. (15) If anyone acknowledges that Jesus is the Son of God, God lives in him and he in God. (16) And so we know and rely on the love God has for us.

God is love. Whoever lives in love lives in God, and God in him. (17) In this way, love is made complete among us so that we will have confidence on the day of judgment, because in this world we are like him. (18) There is no fear in love. But perfect love drives out fear, because fear has to do with punishment. The one who fears is not made perfect in love.

(19) We love because he first loved us. (20) If anyone says, "I love God," yet hates his brother, he is a liar. For anyone who does not love his brother, whom he has seen, cannot love God, whom he has not seen. (21) And he has given us this command: Whoever loves God must also love his brother.

STUFF TO KNOW This verse lays down a huge command. What does God expect you to do (verse 7)?

Suppose you do that—you show love. What does that prove about you (second half of verse 7)? What does it prove if you don't love (verse 8—and verse 20)?

And how does God demonstrate his love for you (verses 9–10)?

DA'SCOOP An "atonement" is making amends for a mistake. That "atoning sacrifice" is one label the Bible uses for Christ's death on the cross. It's the death that paid the penalty for your sins (Romans 6:23) and allows you to be friends with God.

So how does the sacrifice of Jesus set the standard for how you should love people (verse 11)?

What's the payoff if you love like Jesus did (verse 12)?

INSIGHT This Bible Chunk has huge answers for anyone who wants to figure out real love. Verses 7–8 say that love comes from God and that God is love—two facts that are true whether you feel them or not. Verses 9–10 state that God put his love on display for all to see through Jesus' death on the cross. Verses 15–16 say you can be sure of your relationship with God if you acknowledge that Jesus is God's Son. But get this: Verse 12 tells you that *God's love becomes most real when you show God's love to others—and when you let God show you his love through other Christians.*

Utterly important truth: So where does the power to love other people come from (verse 19)?

BIG QUESTIONS If God's goal is for his love to flow *through* you and *to* you from other people, how are you doing—both giving and getting his love?

How could being jammed full of God's love help you love other people better?

DEEP THOT If you want to understand love, you have to get to know God, the ultimate source of love. If you want to stick tight with your friends, you need power from the God who is absolutely stuck on you. And if you want God's love to be totally real in your life, you need to glue yourself to God's people.

STICKY STUFF Remember 1 John 4:19. It tells you where you get the love God wants you to give.

ACT ON IT Spend time with someone who makes God's love real in your life.

DIG ON The Bible can't stop talking about God's love. Check these primo Bible Chunks: Romans 8:38–39, Psalm 86:15, Lamentations 3:22–23, John 3:16, and Romans 5:8.

3. Stewing in a Sewer
(Get godly friends)

As soon as Derek got out of social studies, he race-walked past the crabby hall monitor to the far corner of the library, landing with a thud at a one-person study carrel. See, whenever his day got ugly, Derek had one strategy. He hid. It hadn't occurred to him that the other Christians at school might be able to boost him through life's tough moments. Derek's faith was, well, um, a private thing—no need to talk about it, no need to involve other people, no need to need anything from anyone.

BRAIN DRAIN Why would you want Christian friends?

FLASHBACK Trying to survive as a Christian all by yourself is like crawling into a sewer and pulling the lid shut tight—no light, no warmth, and the situation stinks right from the start. Your faith isn't about you hunkering down with Jesus all by your lonesome. If you read between the lines of this Bible Chunk, you spot a colossal challenge: "You've got God? Then grab hold of this!"

BIBLE CHUNK Read Hebrews 10:19–25

(19) Therefore, brothers, since we have confidence to enter the Most Holy Place by the blood of Jesus, (20) by a new and living way opened for us through the curtain, that is, his body, (21) and since we have a great priest over the house of God, (22) let us draw near to God with a sincere heart in full assurance of faith, having our hearts sprinkled to cleanse us from a guilty conscience and having our bodies washed with pure water. (23) Let us hold unswervingly to the hope we profess, for he who prom-

ised is faithful. (24) And let us consider how we may spur one another on toward love and good deeds. (25) Let us not give up meeting together, as some are in the habit of doing, but let us encourage one another—and all the more as you see the Day approaching.

STUFF TO KNOW What's that first part of this Bible Chunk talking about (verses 19–20)? Any ideas?

SIDELIGHT That "Most Holy Place" was the inner room of the Old Testament temple. It was the closest a human being could get to God's presence. Actually, only the head priest was allowed to slip through a curtain into that room—only once a year—and only if he brought the blood of an animal sacrificed for the people's sins (Leviticus 16). The point? The death of Jesus on the cross opened a way better way for you to get close to God.

Since Jesus did that for you, what do you now have the chance to do (verse 22)?

INSIGHT Having your "heart sprinkled" and "body washed" is what happens when you become God's friend by trusting in Jesus. Your sins are washed away and you stand spanking clean before God.

Watch carefully: The phrase "let us" shows up *five times* in verses 22–25. What's up with that? Look at what you and the Christians in your life are supposed to do—or not do—and finish the phrases:

- (verse 22) Let us . . .

- (verse 23) Let us . . .

- (verse 24) Let us . . .

- (verse 25) Let us *not* . . .

- (verse 25) Let us . . .

INSIGHT Ever wonder what good it will do you to stick tight with Christian friends? Those verses slap you with some good answers: The first two statements challenge you to get close to God and hang on to your faith—together! The third says to prod each other to spiritual growth, using a word that literally means to "irritate" or "exasperate." The fourth reminds you that none of this spiritual growth can happen if you never hang out together. And the fifth says you and your friends have a gargantuan role helping each other keep the faith.

BIG QUESTIONS When has a friend helped you get closer to God? Who? How?

How convinced are you that you actually need Christian friends to get close to God?

SIDELIGHT You can't miss the point that Ecclesiastes 4:9–10, 12 makes about the worth of friends: "Two are better than one, because they have a good return for their work: If one falls down, his friend can help him up. But pity the man who falls and has no one to help him up! Though one may be overpowered, two can defend themselves."

It takes more than you to make an "us." Who in your life is trying to follow those "let us" commands of Hebrews 10 along with you?

DEEP THOT In one breath the Bible tells you Jesus has accomplished something huge for you. In the next breath, God says you need to stick tight to his people. Smells really important.

STICKY STUFF Hebrews 10:24–25 tells you to hang close to your Christian friends.

ACT ON IT Make a list of Christian friends you can rely on to help you grow. If your list comes up short, tell God you want to be an encourager—and that you need some friends to encourage you.

DIG ON John 17 tells you loads more about bonding with your Christian brothers and sisters.

4. Polar Bear Breath
(God wants his love spread around the world)

When Alyssa shows up as a visitor at youth group at a church near her house, everyone knows her. But no one likes her. By the end of the evening, Alyssa realizes the whole group is giving her an icy-cold shoulder—the unwelcoming kind that's so frozen it rips off your lips if you try to kiss up.

BRAIN DRAIN What do you suppose God wants you and your Christian friends to do with all the love you get from him—and the love he intends you to get from each other?

FLASHBACK Some clumps of Christians are like igloos—toasty inside, with a blizzardy chill going on outside. That's not what God intends. Love starts with him. And he intends his warmth to spread not just to Christians but to people who don't know him—people all over the world, in fact. God wants to crack open the igloo and send Christians to the mobs of humanity that need his love. This Bible Chunk comes at the very end of the Bible book of Matthew, so listen up to some of Jesus' final words—words so mightily important that they're called the "Great Commission."

BIBLE CHUNK Read Matthew 28:18–20

(18) Then Jesus came to them and said, "All authority in heaven and on earth has been given to me. (19) Therefore go and make disciples of all nations, baptizing them in the name of the Father and of the Son and of

the Holy Spirit, (20) and teaching them to obey everything I have commanded you. And surely I am with you always, to the very end of the age."

STUFF TO KNOW Halfway through this Bible Chunk

Jesus says "Go!" But he first explains *why* he expects his followers to scoot. What good reason does he give to go (verse 18)?

SIDELIGHT When Jesus rose from the dead, it proved for

all time that his disciples had been hanging out with more than a mere man. Jesus is God's Son, King of the Universe, and the whole world needs to know that fact! Philippians 2:9–11 puts it this way: "Therefore God exalted him to the highest place and gave him the name that is above every name, that at the name of Jesus every knee should bow, in heaven and on earth and under the earth, and every tongue confess that Jesus Christ is Lord, to the glory of God the Father."

Okay. Jesus doesn't hand out road maps and airplane tickets, but where exactly are we supposed to go (verse 19)?

SIDELIGHT "All nations" actually means "all peoples."

God wants to reach not just political nations but the ethnic and language clusters Christian researchers call "people groups." In Acts 1:8 Jesus spells out further *where* we should go. His followers, he says, will take the news of who he is and what he has done from their hometown of Jerusalem out to "the ends of the earth." And in Matthew 5:46–47 and Luke 10:29–37 Jesus says even more about *who* we should go to. Hint: He means everyone around us, including people we might not like.

So when you show up, say, on the outskirts of Ukarumpa—that's in New Guinea—what are you supposed to make (verse 19)? What are you supposed to teach (verse 20)?

INSIGHT You might *want* to go to Ukarumpa. But maybe you'd *rather not*. Here's the big point: Jesus spoke this Bible Chunk to the *church*. He gave us a *group* project to get our heads together and get the job done. To accomplish our task of making disciples— teaching people everywhere to trust and obey Jesus totally—only some of us will travel to people who have never heard of Jesus. But God intends for *all of us* to participate in his global effort by praying (Matthew 9:35–38), giving financial support (2 Corinthians 9:1–14), and warming up the people right around us (Acts 5:42).

Jesus wraps up this possibly-scary assignment with comforting words. What does he promise (verse 20)?

BIG QUESTIONS Bring this back to your life—right here, right now: Do you spread God's love to everyone around you—or do you blast some with an icy exhale that would scare a polar bear? How do you make others feel like they're on the outside looking in?

This Bible Chunk might make you scared. But how does it make you feel that God trusts you with such a crucial assignment?

Who are you going to warm up this week—even if you have to step over the bodies of your frozen Christian friends? How are you going to spread God's love?

DEEP THOT God doesn't give Christians his flaming love just to keep our Christian toes toasty. God's goal is to build an always-expanding group of friends who belong to him—friends who honor him as their Master and rely on his care now and forever, and whose hearts beat with compassion for people near and far. What are you doing to help others experience God's warmth?

STICKY STUFF Cram Matthew 28:19–20 into your cranium.

ACT ON IT Grab a copy of my book *Catch the Wave*, which tells how you can be part of God's plan to warm up the world now and later—and here, there, and everywhere.

DIG ON Look at those Bible Chunks in Matthew 5:46–47 and Luke 10:29–37 to see *who* God wants you to care for.

⑤ Meet the Metalheads
(Non-Christian friends)

Over the past few weeks, Rachel has gotten chummy with Sammy, the girl who sits behind her in math. Their relationship has mostly been about mind-bending geometric proofs, but lately Sammy has started to talk about how scared she is that her dad might leave her mom. But when Rachel mentions her new friendship to her Christian friend Tanner, he explodes. "Sammy? That metalhead? She can't be any good for you. And she's too evil for you to be any good for her. You have to stop talking to her. Tell your teacher to rearrange your seats."

BRAIN DRAIN Do you think Christians should have non-Christian friends? Why—or why not?

FLASHBACK Back in the Old Testament, God told his people to "come out . . . and be pure" from evil nations around them (Isaiah 52:11). In the New Testament, God warns Christians not to be "yoked" with non-Christians (2 Corinthians 6:14), a command that applies most clearly to tight relationships like going out and getting married. But if God wants you to go and make disciples, you can't exactly hide from non-Christians. Jesus' own life offers a huge hint on how to get along with people who don't follow God.

BIBLE CHUNK Read Mark 2:13–17

(13) Once again Jesus went out beside the lake. A large crowd came to him, and he began to teach them. (14) As he walked along, he saw Levi

son of Alphaeus sitting at the tax collector's booth. "Follow me," Jesus told him, and Levi got up and followed him.

(15) While Jesus was having dinner at Levi's house, many tax collectors and "sinners" were eating with him and his disciples, for there were many who followed him. (16) When the teachers of the law who were Pharisees saw him eating with the "sinners" and tax collectors, they asked his disciples: "Why does he eat with tax collectors and 'sinners'?"

(17) On hearing this, Jesus said to them, "It is not the healthy who need a doctor, but the sick. I have not come to call the righteous, but sinners."

STUFF TO KNOW Who all is in the crowd following Jesus? What kind of people are they (verses 13–17)?

INSIGHT You know Levi son of Alphaeus better as Matthew—as in the Bible books of Matthew, Mark, Luke, and John (Matthew 9:9). Matthew was a tax collector, hated by that society as a bottom-feeding life-form—both for cheating people on their taxes and for collaborating with the Roman occupiers of the country. The Pharisees slapped the label "sinner" on anyone who refused to follow the rules as they saw them. And eating with a "sinner" was nearly as bad as taking part in their sin.

So if "the teachers of the law who were Pharisees" regard everyone else as spiritual slime, what do you suppose they think about themselves (verse 16)?

Answer the big question the Pharisees ask: Why does Jesus eat with sinners (verse 17)? Better yet, tell how Jesus responds to that quizzie. . . .

So do you think Jesus is blind to the problems of the people he hangs out with (verse 17)? How do you know?

SIDELIGHT Unlike the Pharisees, the Bible recognizes that *all of us* have wandered from God's path (Isaiah 53:6) and *all of us* are sinners (Romans 3:23). Including people like the Pharisees! Jesus' point is that *all of us* need a spiritual doctor. He never sinned (Hebrews 4:15), but he didn't regard people as beyond healing—or himself as too good to help.

BIG QUESTIONS Jesus calls himself a doctor. What kind of healing is he trying to bring all of us?

What do you think Jesus does when he hangs out with these people? What does he *not* do with them?

Get honest: Why do you have non-Christian friends? Your goal isn't to lop off people who aren't hot prospects for becoming Christians—but is helping your non-Christian friends get to know Jesus part of your plan?

When would a friendship with a non-Christian get in the way of your following God?

Say it in your own words: What does this Bible Chunk say about what kind of non-Christian friends you should have—and why?

DEEP THOT Jesus was a spiritual doctor. He wasn't afraid to dive into the gory mess of people's lives. But his aim was to heal—not to get in on their sin. What's your goal?

STICKY STUFF Mark 2:17 tells you who you're aiming to help.

ACT ON IT Get together with a mature Christian friend to decide on one or two non-Christians you want to do your best to demonstrate God's love to. Talk too about whether any of your current friendships with non-Christians are sucking you where you shouldn't go.

DIG ON Flip to John 4:1–42 for another glimpse of how Jesus treated someone religious folks rejected.

Talk About It • 1

EMPATHIZE: What's going on in your life?
ENCOURAGE: How are you doing with Jesus?
EQUIP: What one truth will you take home today?

- What would you like the crowds at your school to do to prove your wild popularity? (Study 1)
- Do you think it's possible for a Christian to be tightly connected to people and God at the same time? Why or why not? (Study 1)
- In your real world, how might friends get in the way of following God? (Study 1)
- How would you answer someone who says she's never felt loved? (Study 2)
- How can being jammed full of God's love help you love other people better? (Study 2)
- Are you convinced that you need Christian friends? Why or why not? (Study 3)
- What does God want you and your Christian friends to do with all the love you get from him? (Study 4)
- Do you spread God's love to everyone around you—or do you make others feel like they're on the outside looking in? What proof do you see in your life? (Study 4)
- Do you think Christians should have non-Christian friends? Why or why not? (Study 5)
- How is helping non-Christian friends get to know Jesus part of your life? (Study 5)

PART 2

A FRIEND
WORTH
HAVING

6. Tangling With Toe Jam
(Being a servant)

Chad thought he had the friendship thing all figured out. Outside, his house had a multilevel swimming pool—inside, a not-so-mini arcade and an eye-popping, ear-bursting home theater system. With playthings like that, he figured he'd be a friend magnet. And he was right. He had a waiting list of classmates who wanted to hang out with him.

BRAIN DRAIN What's the best way to get friends?

FLASHBACK You probably don't have the option of giving away major cash or prizes to make friends—but maybe you wish you did. Jesus, though, shows an even more dazzling, durable way to win friends. As the clock ticks down the final hours before his crucifixion, he demonstrates for his followers what this Bible Chunk calls "the full extent of his love." Then he commands us to act the same way. If you want to be a friend worth having, Jesus shows you how.

BIBLE CHUNK Read John 13:1-17

(1) It was just before the Passover Feast. Jesus knew that the time had come for him to leave this world and go to the Father. Having loved his own who were in the world, he now showed them the full extent of his love.

(2) The evening meal was being served, and the devil had already prompted Judas Iscariot, son of Simon, to betray Jesus. (3) Jesus knew that the Father had put all things under his power, and that he had come

from God and was returning to God; (4) so he got up from the meal, took off his outer clothing, and wrapped a towel around his waist. (5) After that, he poured water into a basin and began to wash his disciples' feet, drying them with the towel that was wrapped around him.

(6) He came to Simon Peter, who said to him, "Lord, are you going to wash my feet?"

(7) Jesus replied, "You do not realize now what I am doing, but later you will understand."

(8) "No," said Peter, "you shall never wash my feet."

Jesus answered, "Unless I wash you, you have no part with me."

(9) "Then, Lord," Simon Peter replied, "not just my feet but my hands and my head as well!"

(10) Jesus answered, "A person who has had a bath needs only to wash his feet; his whole body is clean. And you are clean, though not every one of you." (11) For he knew who was going to betray him, and that was why he said not every one was clean.

(12) When he had finished washing their feet, he put on his clothes and returned to his place. "Do you understand what I have done for you?" he asked them. (13) "You call me 'Teacher' and 'Lord,' and rightly so, for that is what I am. (14) Now that I, your Lord and Teacher, have washed your feet, you also should wash one another's feet. (15) I have set you an example that you should do as I have done for you. (16) I tell you the truth, no servant is greater than his master, nor is a messenger greater than the one who sent him. (17) Now that you know these things, you will be blessed if you do them.

STUFF TO KNOW What way-out thing did Jesus do to show love to his closest friends (verse 5)? Why do that?

INSIGHT Jesus' disciples were burly guys who trudged dusty roads wearing sandals—a sure path to grungy, malodorous feet. By untying their sandals and rinsing the dirt from their feet, Jesus performed a practical, necessary deed. But foot washing, a task none of the disciples would willingly stoop to, was the job of a servant. By the way—the account of this event in the Bible book of Luke mentions that the disciples had just been arguing about which one of them was the greatest (Luke 22:24).

Peter fusses. Jesus flings it back at him. What are they arguing about (verses 6–10)?

INSIGHT In a roundabout way, Jesus is saying that Peter is already his friend and follower, so he doesn't need a whole-body spiritual cleansing to get right with him. Jesus just wants Peter to experience a real-life act of humble love as he bows to wash his feet. Peter doesn't get it.

So what does Jesus expect his followers to do (verse 14)?

And what does Jesus promise people who follow his command (verse 17)?

BIG QUESTIONS Jesus is God. King of the Universe. Ruler of All. How does someone of that huge stature usually demand to be treated?

Do you think that Jesus' approach—taking the role of a servant—is the right way to make and maintain friends? Why or why not?

SIDELIGHT Jesus isn't obsessed with toe jam. Philippians 2:3–4 talks about what servanthood does and doesn't mean—and it details God's design for friendship: "Do nothing out of selfish ambition or vain conceit, but in humility consider others better than yourselves. Each of you should look not only to your own interests, but also to the interests of others." Being a servant doesn't mean you put yourself down—but that you put others up. That's an attitude people find attractive—and one God promises to bless.

DEEP THOT How would you like a collection of friends who care about your needs as much as they care about their own? That's the kind of love that sticks people together forever. If you grow in showing that Christlike mind-set toward other people, you won't ever have to buy friends. People will beg to be around you.

STICKY STUFF Remember Christ's unforgettable example in John 13:14–15. There's a card in the back, as always.

ACT ON IT Do something today that shows honor to another person by putting his or her interests before yours.

DIG ON Read Philippians 2:1–11 for more on Jesus' style of servanthood.

7. Dealing With the Nitty-Gritty

(The qualities of a friend)

When the most drop-dead gorgeous girl in school grabs the seat across from Josh at lunch, his heart thumps so hard it almost explodes out of his chest and blows vessels in his brain. "You're not like everyone else," Shelli blurts. "You're real. You don't trash-talk people. Most guys are potty-mouths. They don't know how to treat girls. I don't understand you. Are you a fake?"

BRAIN DRAIN Do you think it's possible to be good without making people gag? Why or why not?

FLASHBACK The nitty-gritty qualities of being a friend worth having aren't just about being nice. They aren't charms you flip on to wow the hotties in your world. And they aren't a surfacey disguise you can plaster on like makeup. You only get those qualities when you let God radically remake your life. Right before this Bible Chunk, Paul reminds his readers not to live like people who still pursue evil. Those folks, Paul says, "are hopelessly confused. Their closed minds are full of darkness; they are far away from the life of God because they have shut their minds and hardened their hearts against him. They don't care anymore about right and wrong . . ." (Ephesians 4:17–19 NLT). Your job as a Christian is to ditch those dark ways and become a friend who shocks people with the genuine goodness of your attitudes and actions. Here's what that looks like.

BIBLE CHUNK Read Ephesians 4:25–5:10

(4:25) Therefore each of you must put off falsehood and speak truthfully to his neighbor, for we are all members of one body. (4:26) "In your anger do not sin": Do not let the sun go down while you are still angry, (4:27) and do not give the devil a foothold. (4:28) He who has been stealing must steal no longer, but must work, doing something useful with his own hands, that he may have something to share with those in need.

(4:29) Do not let any unwholesome talk come out of your mouths, but only what is helpful for building others up according to their needs, that it may benefit those who listen. (4:30) And do not grieve the Holy Spirit of God, with whom you were sealed for the day of redemption. (4:31) Get rid of all bitterness, rage and anger, brawling and slander, along with every form of malice. (4:32) Be kind and compassionate to one another, forgiving each other, just as in Christ God forgave you.

(5:1) Be imitators of God, therefore, as dearly loved children (5:2) and live a life of love, just as Christ loved us and gave himself up for us as a fragrant offering and sacrifice to God.

(5:3) But among you there must not be even a hint of sexual immorality, or of any kind of impurity, or of greed, because these are improper for God's holy people. (5:4) Nor should there be obscenity, foolish talk or coarse joking, which are out of place, but rather thanksgiving. (5:5) For of this you can be sure: No immoral, impure or greedy person—such a man is an idolater—has any inheritance in the kingdom of Christ and of God. (5:6) Let no one deceive you with empty words, for because of such things God's wrath comes on those who are disobedient. (5:7) Therefore do not be partners with them. (5:8) For you were once darkness, but now you are light in the Lord. Live as children of light (5:9) (for the fruit of the light consists in all goodness, righteousness and truth) (5:10) and find out what pleases the Lord.

STUFF TO KNOW This Bible Chunk contains a load

of things to ditch—and to do. You probably already do great at some of these, but other commands might feel like a poke in your conscience. Look again at each of these verses, get honest with yourself, and jot down one change you want God to help you make in each of these areas to make you a better friend:

- Put off falsehood and speak truth (verse 4:26)

- Don't let the sun set on your anger (verses 4:26–27)

- Don't mooch (verse 4:28)

- Speak words that build up (verse 4:29)

- Pay attention to the Holy Spirit (verse 4:30)

- Do away with ugly mood swings (verse 4:31)

- Show kindness (verse 4:32)

- Stay sexually pure (verse 5:3)

- Don't wish for what belongs to someone else (verse 5:3)

- Ditch dirty words (verse 5:4)

One last thought: Who are you supposed to imitate? How come (verses 5:1–2)?

BIG QUESTIONS Suppose someone wants to snap a picture of your life. What's your best side? Where do you do best in being God's kind of friend?

So in imitating God, living a life of love, and being a fantastic friend, what's your biggest struggle?

How do you figure God will help you change? What do verses 5:1–2 have to do with it?

DEEP THOT You might stare at that list of what a mature Christian friend looks like and feel like you're a million miles away from that goal. But it's where God wants you to go. And if you let him, he *will* remake you. Keep your heart open to him (Ephesians 4:17–19).

STICKY STUFF Remember Ephesians 5:1–2—and remind yourself who loves you and gives you power to love others.

ACT ON IT Memorize a couple more verses that challenge you to be a better friend.

DIG ON Check out Philippians 1:6, where God promises to complete the huge remaking job he's begun in you.

8. Your Pain, Their Gain
(Comforting your friends)

When Tara's dad fell sick with cancer, slid into a coma, and died, Jamal was the only person who could get through to Tara. She listened quietly to what Jamal said, chewing on every word. Jamal's own dad, after all, had died a couple years before—but of a heart attack. Tara and Jamal spent long hours talking about how bad the whole thing hurt, how life would change, and how they could survive. To be honest, Tara would have crumpled into a lump of permanent sadness if he hadn't been around.

BRAIN DRAIN When has a friend helped you through something painful—major or minor? How did he or she know how to help?

FLASHBACK Paul often starts his Bible letters with a longish prayer for his readers, like in Colossians 1:3–12. When he starts his letter to the Corinthians by asking them to pray for *him*, you can be sure he's been through a massively painful experience. But look at what he does with those hurts.

BIBLE CHUNK Read 2 Corinthians 1:3–11

(3) Praise be to the God and Father of our Lord Jesus Christ, the Father of compassion and the God of all comfort, (4) who comforts us in all our troubles, so that we can comfort those in any trouble with the comfort we ourselves have received from God. (5) For just as the sufferings of Christ flow over into our lives, so also through Christ our comfort overflows. (6) If we are distressed, it is for your comfort and salvation; if we are com-

forted, it is for your comfort, which produces in you patient endurance of the same sufferings we suffer. (7) And our hope for you is firm, because we know that just as you share in our sufferings, so also you share in our comfort.

(8) We do not want you to be uninformed, brothers, about the hardships we suffered in the province of Asia. We were under great pressure, far beyond our ability to endure, so that we despaired even of life. (9) Indeed, in our hearts we felt the sentence of death. But this happened that we might not rely on ourselves but on God, who raises the dead. (10) He has delivered us from such a deadly peril, and he will deliver us. On him we have set our hope that he will continue to deliver us, (11) as you help us by your prayers. Then many will give thanks on our behalf for the gracious favor granted us in answer to the prayers of many.

STUFF TO KNOW Lots of folks see God as a smoke-spewing meanie. But what does this Bible Chunk call him (verse 3)?

What does God do to care for you when life gets ghastly (verses 4–5)?

If you followed Paul's example, what would you do with the help God gives you when you suffer (verses 4, 6)?

INSIGHT A nasty situation won't suddenly feel nice just because you know you can pass on to other hurting people everything you're learning. But it's a fact that you usually get a chance to take what you suffer and turn it around for someone else's good. Paul boldly believes that whatever happens to him—good or bad—will benefit others. He also points out that whatever suffering comes his way for being a Christian, God has an even bigger heap of comfort.

DA'SCOOP Comfort isn't just patting someone on the back until she feels better. It means coming to someone's side to relieve pain and anxiety. It's help, consolation, and encouragement. Often you provide comfort by just listening.

Does it sound like Paul's life had been really happy lately (verse 8)? How bad was it (verses 8–9)?

INSIGHT The "province of Asia" Paul talks about isn't any-where near China. It's in modern-day Turkey, a few hundred miles from his readers in Corinth, Greece.

What other lesson has Paul gained from his experience (verse 9)?

SIDELIGHT Paul isn't just talking about trivial pains. In 2 Corinthians 11:23–29 you can read about other hurts he suf-fered—everything from shipwrecks to stonings.

BIG QUESTIONS What are the toughest things you've faced in life?

Have you gotten hold of God's comfort for those situations? How have God and other people helped you?

If you have gotten comfort in those situations, then what kind of comfort can you offer other hurting people—people in the same or similar circumstances? Who needs your help right now?

DEEP THOT Hardly anyone in a tough situation likes to hear that God will use their pain for someone else's gain. But once you can look back and see how God stuck with you through it all, then you might be ready to comfort others with the comfort he gave you. Turning hurts into help is what friends do.

ACT ON IT Comfort doesn't mean banging people on the head with the raw facts of God's care. It means getting into their hurt and giving them what they need most—help, consolation, encouragement. Find someone to comfort today.

STICKY STUFF Second Corinthians 1:3–4 shows you how to stick close to your friends when life gets hard.

DIG ON Read about God's comfort in Psalm 46:1–3.

9. Appreciating Rat-Boy
(You have gifts to offer your world)

He is so misunderstood. Everyone calls him Rat-Boy. He doesn't have rats. He has mice. Okay, so Rat-Boy can't throw a football. Rat-Boy can't dance. Rat-Boy can't find his way from one end of the school building to the other. But his large-scale, still-in-high-school study of mice raised on contaminated river water might just force polluters to clean the stream. Or even someday save the planet.

BRAIN DRAIN What hidden talent do you have to offer the world?

FLASHBACK A few of the "spiritual gifts" talked about in this Bible Chunk cause gigantic controversy among Christians. But the point of the passage is that God has given each Christian special gifts to proclaim his Good News, show off his goodness, and exclaim his greatness—all so that his kingdom is built up. Some gifts look very everydayish. Others are mind-blowingly spectacular. But all of these gifts seem to go above and beyond the talents God wired into you at the factory and the abilities you polish through training. The whole package of what God has put inside you is what you have to offer the world.

BIBLE CHUNK Read 1 Corinthians 12:1, 4–11

(1) Now about spiritual gifts, brothers, I do not want you to be ignorant. . . .

(4) There are different kinds of gifts, but the same Spirit. (5) There are

different kinds of service, but the same Lord. (6) There are different kinds of working, but the same God works all of them in all men.

(7) Now to each one the manifestation of the Spirit is given for the common good. (8) To one there is given through the Spirit the message of wisdom, to another the message of knowledge by means of the same Spirit, (9) to another faith by the same Spirit, to another gifts of healing by that one Spirit, (10) to another miraculous powers, to another prophecy, to another distinguishing between spirits, to another speaking in different kinds of tongues, and to still another the interpretation of tongues. (11) All these are the work of one and the same Spirit, and he gives them to each one, just as he determines.

STUFF TO KNOW Big point: Are all these "spiritual gifts" thingies the same? Another way to ask that: Do they all look the same when they are used to serve God (verses 4–6)?

Who dishes out these gifts (verse 7)?

Double-check your answer against verse 11, then answer this: So is anybody left out when God hands out gifts (verse 11)?

And who decides *which* gift or gifts you get (verse 11)?

What are you supposed to do with your gift? Who is it supposed to benefit (verse 7)?

INSIGHT In verses 8–11 Paul catalogs some of the gifts God gives—and there are other gift lists in 1 Corinthians 14:1–30, Ephesians 4:11–13, and Romans 12:4–8. The point in each list? Each ability is *uniquely valuable* and *absolutely necessary.*

SIDELIGHT Spiritual gifts are only one part of the package of God's gifts to you. Look at the apostle Paul, for example. He had the spiritual gift of apostleship (Romans 1:1), which is the twin ability to lead multiple churches and to declare the Good News across cultures. He also had a talent for tentmaking that determined where he would preach (Acts 18:1–4). He had a personality unafraid of conflict (Galatians 2:1–15). And he had a passion to preach where no one else had preached before (2 Corinthians 10:16). You too have a great mix of gifts inside you.

BIG QUESTIONS What gifts has God given you—not just spiritual gifts, but all sorts? What are you good at?

Do you ever get knotted up with jealousy and wish you had someone else's assortment of gifts?

SIDELIGHT Galatians 6:4 says to keep your eyes on your own actions—and take pride in yourself, not comparing yourself to others.

Stretch your brain: How can you use the qualities that make you uniquely you to build up your friends—and pull them closer to God?

DEEP THOT
God don't give dumb gifts. Next to Jesus, the biggest gift you can give your friends is *you*. As American poet e.e. cummings wrote, "The hardest battle is to be nobody but yourself in a world which is doing its best, night and day, to make you everybody else." Do you really think that God could use your gifts to do good in this world? Why not?

STICKY STUFF
Be sure that you have gifts—and that God has a plan for you to use them. Memorize 1 Corinthians 12:7.

ACT ON IT
If you have a hard time identifying and appreciating your incredible giftedness, grab a copy of *Find Your Fit*, the youth version of the adult book *LifeKeys* and a book I co-wrote with human resources whiz Jane Kise. You'll never look down on yourself again.

DIG ON
You've got to grab a look at 1 Corinthians 12:14–26, where Paul does a comic riff on how all our different gifts work together in the church, just like the parts of the body.

(10.) Mob Mentality
(Standing up to your peers)

Janessa couldn't believe it when her two best friends told her to quit reading her Bible during study breaks at the library. They said it made *them* look bad—and it made *her* look like some religious freakazoid. Janessa wasn't trying to start a scene, make a point, or look holier than the rest of the library. She was even using her ultra-slim, ultra-inconspicuous New Testament. She was just reading—and praying without moving her lips. She knew she had every right to open her Bible—and to shut her eyes. What was their problem?

BRAIN DRAIN When have you had to stand up to what people thought of you—for being a Christian or for anything else?

FLASHBACK This is a hugely important Bible Chunk. You see Paul standing up for the core of Christian belief—the truth that God has offered to save and bring to heaven all who trust that his Son, Jesus Christ, died for their sins. Weirdly, Paul has to resist the pressure of people who are supposed to be Christians. Whether someone puts a gun to your head to force you to give up your faith—or you just want to obey God in something a lot less heroic—Paul coaches you to please God, not to pacify your peers.

BIBLE CHUNK Read Galatians 1:3–10

(3) Grace and peace to you from God our Father and the Lord Jesus Christ, (4) who gave himself for our sins to rescue us from the present evil

age, according to the will of our God and Father, (5) to whom be glory for ever and ever. Amen.

(6) I am astonished that you are so quickly deserting the one who called you by the grace of Christ and are turning to a different gospel— (7) which is really no gospel at all. Evidently some people are throwing you into confusion and are trying to pervert the gospel of Christ. (8) But even if we or an angel from heaven should preach a gospel other than the one we preached to you, let him be eternally condemned! (9) As we have already said, so now I say again: If anybody is preaching to you a gospel other than what you accepted, let him be eternally condemned!

(10) Am I now trying to win the approval of men, or of God? Or am I trying to please men? If I were still trying to please men, I would not be a servant of Christ.

STUFF TO KNOW What's Paul talking about at the start of this Bible Chunk (verses 3–4)?

DA'SCOOP That "grace" stuff is God's unmerited favor— the love he shows us, which as evildoers we don't deserve (Romans 5:8). Paul hits right up front the fact he's going to fight for: Jesus alone is the one who died to rescue us from evil, setting us free from the penalty and power of sin.

What dumb thing are the people in Galatia doing (verse 6)?

What does Paul think of the Galatian folks' fake "gospel" (verse 7)?

INSIGHT The rest of this Bible book—especially chapter 3— unpacks the wacked-out belief the Galatians are following: They think they can earn God's love by keeping rules. Fact is, Christians

keep God's commands because they are *already* loved by him. The Galatians have totally ditched the truth. Not only that, they are ditching God himself, the one who invites them to be his friends for free.

What does Paul say should happen to someone who preaches anything less than the accurate Gospel (verses 8–9)?

INSIGHT Fierce words. Paul is inviting God to roast in hell anyone who preaches anything short of the true Gospel.

Here's the big point: Why is Paul so stuck on the truth of his message? Who is he trying to keep happy (verse 10)?

SIDELIGHT In Acts 5:28–29 some religious teachers threatened to jail the early Christians if they preached Christ. The Christians knew whom they had to obey: "We must obey God rather than men!" When you're forced to choose between pleasing God and pleasing people, there's no contest.

BIG QUESTIONS How much are your attitudes and actions influenced by your peers? When have you put your friends' demands before God's commands? Back up your answer with *facts*.

Why isn't Paul any too nice on this one point? Do you think it's okay for Christians to stand up for something as fiercely as he did? Why or why not?

When you choose what God wants over what friends want, does taking God's side make you any less of a friend? Explain.

DEEP THOT God is King of the Universe and Lord of your life. You owe him total obedience. But that doesn't mean you love your friends any less. Jesus said you should "let your light shine before men, that they may see your good deeds and praise your Father in heaven" (Matthew 5:16). Sometimes the best friend you can be is someone who stands against the crowd and points the way to what's right.

ACT ON IT Ask a mature Christian to let you know if he or she ever spots you caving in to peer pressure.

STICKY STUFF Stick Galatians 1:10 in your head and stick up for what's right.

DIG ON Ever feel pummeled by your peers—and tempted to go along with whatever they want? Give Luke 12:4–12 a look.

Talk About It • 2

EMPATHIZE: What's going on in your life?
ENCOURAGE: How are you doing with Jesus?
EQUIP: What one truth will you take home today?

- What's the best way to get friends? (Study 6)
- Do you think that Jesus' approach—taking the role of a servant—is the right way to make and maintain friends? Why or why not? (Study 6)
- Is it possible to be good without making people gag? How? (Study 7)
- In imitating God—living a life of love—where do you do best? Where do you struggle? (Study 7)
- When has a friend helped you through something painful—major or minor? What did he or she do to help? (Study 8)
- How can you help people with the stuff you've learned in the tough circumstances of life? (Study 8)
- What talents do you have to offer the world? (Study 9)
- How can you use your gifts to pull friends closer to God? (Study 9)
- When have you had to stand up to what people thought of you—for being a Christian or anything else? (Study 10)
- When have you put your friends' demands before God's commands? Does taking God's side make you any less of a friend? Explain. (Study 10)

PART 3

THE BEST
FRIENDS
YOU CAN
FIND

⑪ Live-wired
(How to find the best friends)

Katie's friends were totally puzzled when they discovered her prom date was a dead guy. "Oh, he's the best," she reassured them. "He's a little stiff, but he never stops smiling. And he's a great listener. You should have seen us—he was so cute when he picked me up. His parents stuffed his tuxedo jacket with money and pinned a note on him to tell the chauffeur where to take us. I wouldn't trade him for anything."

BRAIN DRAIN How much fun would it be to be best friends with a dead guy?

FLASHBACK No doubt you want the most excellent friends you can find. If your goal is to glom with people who can help you get close to God, then your best bets aren't the ones all gussied up on the outside, propped up in the back of a limo. You can do better. You want friends whose insides are alive.

BIBLE CHUNK Read Ephesians 2:1–10

(1) As for you, you were dead in your transgressions and sins, (2) in which you used to live when you followed the ways of this world and of the ruler of the kingdom of the air, the spirit who is now at work in those who are disobedient. (3) All of us also lived among them at one time, gratifying the cravings of our sinful nature and following its desires and thoughts. Like the rest, we were by nature objects of wrath. (4) But because of his great love for us, God, who is rich in mercy, (5) made us alive with Christ even when we were dead in transgressions—it is by grace you

have been saved. (6) And God raised us up with Christ and seated us with him in the heavenly realms in Christ Jesus, (7) in order that in the coming ages he might show the incomparable riches of his grace, expressed in his kindness to us in Christ Jesus. (8) For it is by grace you have been saved, through faith—and this not from yourselves, it is the gift of God—(9) not by works, so that no one can boast. (10) For we are God's workmanship, created in Christ Jesus to do good works, which God prepared in advance for us to do.

STUFF TO KNOW In this second chapter of his letter to the Ephesians, Paul starts off by talking about what all of us human beings are like before we know God. What's he say (verse 1)?

Who do folks follow when they don't know God (verse 2)?

SIDELIGHT That doesn't mean everyone on earth is a Satan-worshiper—well, not exactly. Know it or not, all sinners are part of Satan's global rebellion against God (look back at Genesis 3). And here's a killer—how did we use to act (verse 3)?

Verse 4 says our sinful actions made us targets of God's anger. But what did he do instead of smoking us—all because of his incredible love for us (verses 4–5)?

INSIGHT Without God, even people dressed to kill are still

dead in their disobedience to God. But when folks become Christians, God freely forgives them. He makes them his friends and jump-starts their hearts. Once they were dead toward God. Now they're "alive with Christ." They start to follow the one who saved them.

Don't miss one last point: Why did God make us his friends (tail end of verse 5, and verses 8–9)?

INSIGHT That's the grace thingie you read about last time. God saves us not based on "works"—marvelous things we do—but because he chooses to be merciful. He saves us when we put our trust in Jesus and everything he's done for us.

BIG QUESTIONS So how is trying to get life from a non-Christian like dating a dead guy—or girl? What kind of life can your Christian friends offer you that non-Christian friends can't?

INSIGHT Your Christian friends might never be the life of the party. But they have something better to offer: They're connected to the Life-giver. And they're filled with a one-of-a-kind love of God you won't find in your non-Christian friends.

When have you felt encouraged—tapped into God—from hanging tight with Christian friends?

Does that mean Christians always make absolutely flawless friends?

INSIGHT When someone first gets to know God, you might not see much life right away—you can't see evidence of God when it's just started on the inside. But God's good stuff doesn't take long to ooze to the outside—and you start to spot changed thoughts, words, and actions. Sooner or later that will spill out on you.

DEEP THOT You can't escape the fact that God wants you to have Christian friends (John 17:20–23). You can't dodge his command to get together and grow (Hebrews 10:25). If your goal is to glue yourself to godly friends, then you have to know how to find them in the first place. And you spot a Christian by the new life that's begun. Life grows. Life shows.

ACT ON IT Make a list of your closest friends. Think through that list: Which friends are sharing the life of God with you? What are you going to do about getting friends who give you life?

STICKY STUFF Ephesians 2:4–5 reminds you how God has zapped life into his friends.

DIG ON Check out Acts 2:42–47 to see how the first Christians grew together.

12. Friends Again
(God's definition of being a Christian)

"I mean, how do *you* know who is and isn't a Christian?" Michael huffed at Saleena, who'd been trying for a long time to tell him about Jesus. "It's so rude to think *you* know who is connected to God. My neighbor is into Druid stuff. He's way more spiritual than a lot of people who claim to be Christians."

BRAIN DRAIN Would it be snobbish—or worse—to make it your aim to find Christian friends? Why or why not?

FLASHBACK The Bible declares that people get close to God only through Jesus. Like it says right before this Bible Chunk, "And through Christ, God has brought all things back to himself again—things on earth and things in heaven. God made peace through the blood of Christ's death on the cross" (Colossians 1:20 NCV). God never made it your job to bash people who don't believe in him. But the Bible is blunt that real Christians pass this crucial test: They are *reconciled to God*.

BIBLE CHUNK Read Colossians 1:21–23

(21) Once you were alienated from God and were enemies in your minds because of your evil behavior. (22) But now he has reconciled you by Christ's physical body through death to present you holy in his sight, without blemish and free from accusation—(23) if you continue in your faith, established and firm, not moved from the hope held out in the gospel. This is the gospel that you heard and that has been proclaimed to every creature under heaven, and of which I, Paul, have become a servant.

STUFF TO KNOW Think back—if you remember—
to your before-you-believed-in-Jesus days. Why were you a long
ways from God? What are people like before they know God
(verse 21)?

SIDELIGHT If you're like every other human on earth—
and you are—you started as an enemy of God. You most likely
weren't a mass murderer, but your thoughts and behavior missed
God's totally holy standards. Romans 3:10–11 says, "There is no
one righteous, not even one; there is no one who understands, no
one who seeks God."

That would be nasty news—except for what Christ did. How did he
fix your relationship with God (verse 22)?

What does God think of you once you have been reconciled
through Christ's death (verse 22)?

DA'SCOOP You might be hazy on what "reconcile" pre-
cisely means. It's to "reestablish a close relationship." It comes
from the word "conciliate," which means to "overcome distrust"
or "to regain good will." Jesus' death is what reconciles us to God.

One last one. "Gospel" means "good news." What's so good about
the news of what Jesus has done (verse 23)?

BIG QUESTIONS Here's a huge one for you: Do you feel like God's friend? What makes you sure—or not sure?

INSIGHT These three verses sum up how you get straight with God. Take a look at them in the easy-to-read *New Century Version* of the Bible:

- Apart from Jesus, all people have a PROBLEM (verse 21): "At one time you were separated from God. You were his enemies in your minds, and the evil things you did were against God."
- God has a SOLUTION (verse 22): "But now God has made you his friends again. He did this through Christ's death in the body so that he might bring you into God's presence as people who are holy, with no wrong, and with nothing of which God can judge you guilty."
- And there's a right RESPONSE (verse 23) to make to God's SO-LUTION to your PROBLEM: "This will happen if you continue strong and sure in your faith. You must not be moved away from the hope brought to you by the Good News that you heard."

Belief in this "Good News" isn't just "Yeah, I agree with that in my head." Having "faith" (verse 23) means you can say "I trust my life to that." Have you responded to God's solution to your problem with that kind of faith? Have your friends?

INSIGHT Maybe you grew up trusting that Jesus died for your sins—or maybe you've never really grabbed hold of God's Good News and you want to talk to him about it now. For you or any of those non-Christians around you to become a Christian is as straightforward as telling God something like this: "God, I know I've wronged you. I trust that Jesus died for my sins. Thank you for making me your friend, and help me stick close to you." When you believe in Jesus—when you accept who he is and what he has done for you—you change from being God's enemy to being God's friend. You're reconciled.

If that's *God's* standard for what it means to be a Christian, what does that have to do with spotting Christian friends?

DEEP THOT Don't be deceived. God's true friends are the people who are reconciled to God through Christ. And they're the ones you can share his life with.

STICKY STUFF Colossians 1:21–22 is the core of your faith, so pop it into your cerebrum and cork it so it doesn't ooze out.

ACT ON IT Tell a friend how you've responded to God's solution to your problem.

DIG ON Check out Colossians 1:13–14 for another way to describe what it means to become God's friends.

13. Aromas Up Your Nose
(Christians are being remade)

After yet another verbal skirmish at home, your parents conclude that you're getting thrashed by the nasties of life. You need to re-invent yourself, they figure, so they ship you to a month-long spa. You get cucumbers on your eyelids, mudpacks on your face, and aromas up your nose. You roast on a tanning bed like a chicken on a spit. And you pump through a triathlete-training regimen. Yet when you blow up at your family on your first day back, everyone knows you haven't changed a bit. You're buff. You're beautiful. But you're still a crab.

BRAIN DRAIN If you could change anything about yourself, what would it be?

FLASHBACK Most people on planet Earth could stand a spin in a spa. But the potential rejuvenation and revitalization amounts to nothing compared to the work God does in you. Once you're reconciled to God, you don't just get relaxed—you get re-made. This Bible Chunk contains two words telling how that happens. *Grace*, you know, is our undeserved favor from God. It's the motive behind all of God's forgiveness, friendship, and fatherliness. And *salvation* is the name for this package of everything God does to rescue you from sin and build a relationship with you.

BIBLE CHUNK Read Titus 2:11–15

(11) For the grace of God that brings salvation has appeared to all men.
(12) It teaches us to say "No" to ungodliness and worldly passions, and to

live self-controlled, upright and godly lives in this present age, (13) while we wait for the blessed hope—the glorious appearing of our great God and Savior, Jesus Christ, (14) who gave himself for us to redeem us from all wickedness and to purify for himself a people that are his very own, eager to do what is good.

(15) These, then, are the things you should teach. Encourage and rebuke with all authority. Do not let anyone despise you.

STUFF TO KNOW So what does God's grace train you to say "no" to (verse 12)?

DA'SCOOP "Ungodliness" is the ugly attitude that God doesn't matter in life—and all the evil actions that result when you ignore God and his commands. "Worldly passions" are cravings to do what's wrong.

What sort of life does God's grace teach you to say "yes" to (verse 12)?

DA'SCOOP Get this: God wants to grow you three ways: He wants to remake you to be "self-controlled" (to act rightly toward yourself), "upright" (toward others), and "godly" (toward him).

Why does God want to free you from "all wickedness," to yank you out of doing evil and help you decide to do good (verse 14)?

SIDELIGHT Second Corinthians 5:15 makes that point in slightly different words: "He died for everyone so that those who

receive his new life will no longer live to please themselves. Instead, they will live to please Christ, who died and was raised for them" (NLT). God gives you the privilege of living for him for his glory and for your good.

BIG QUESTIONS Explain in your own words what it means to be remade by God.

How would you feel if you were Titus and God told you "these are the things you should teach," like in verse 15? How would you explain to your friends that you think it's worth it to say "no" to ungodliness?

SIDELIGHT You probably don't see yourself as a preacher. But actually, that's a message God wants you to say and keep saying to your Christian friends. Hebrews 3:13 puts it this way: "You must warn each other every day. . . so that none of you will be deceived by sin and hardened against God" (NLT). More on that in study 15.

Suppose you have a friend who knows Christ but doesn't ever think about growing spiritually—getting remade in how he acts toward himself, others, or God. Would you pick that person as a really close friend? Why or why not?

INSIGHT In 2 Timothy 2:22 Paul told a youngish Timothy of the best friends he could aim for. "But run away from the evil young people like to do," he wrote. "Try hard to live right and to have faith, love, and peace, together with those who trust in the

Lord from pure hearts" (NCV). You can settle for less, or aim for God's best.

Who do you know who is gonzo about growing in God? Do you want that person as a close friend? What holds you back?

DEEP THOT People who belong to God are reconciled. They're being remade. They're also responsive—more on that next time. Do your own deep thinking: What kind of friends are you wanting right about now?

STICKY STUFF Ponder what could happen in you and your Christian friends if you kept Titus 2:11–12 in the forefront of your brain.

ACT ON IT Who do you know who wants to be remade by God? Talk to them about your desire to grow with God.

DIG ON Read Matthew 13:44–45 to find out about people smart enough to know the value of following God totally.

(14.) Getting Up After You Mess Up
(Being responsive to God)

Twenty-three guys brilliant enough to set a new camp record for people standing on a top bunk should have known the fun couldn't last. And when the bunk splatted and splintered, guys scattered. No one wanted any part of the blame: "It wasn't my bunk." "I wasn't the one who bounced. I was just standing there." "I didn't know the bunk would break." "It's the stupid bunk's fault." But there were two guys who admitted they'd done the damage—and offered to pay their part to replace the bunk.

BRAIN DRAIN How quick are you to admit you're wrong? Examples, please!

FLASHBACK Know it or not, having the guts to say you're wrong is one of the basic steps of being a Christian. It's at the root of repenting and coming to God. You might be quick to confess. Or you might stubbornly hold to your innocence or have an ugly habit of ratting on others. You can spot the same tendencies—good or bad—in potential friends. And real friends, by the way, aren't people who never do anything wrong. They're the people who know how to make things right.

BIBLE CHUNK Read 1 John 1:8–2:2

(1:8) If we claim to be without sin, we deceive ourselves and the truth is not in us. (1:9) If we confess our sins, he is faithful and just and will forgive us our sins and purify us from all unrighteousness. (1:10) If we claim we have not sinned, we make him out to be a liar and his word has no place in our lives. (2:1) My dear children, I write this to you so that you will not sin. But if anybody does sin, we have one who speaks to the Father in our defense—Jesus Christ, the Righteous One. (2:2) He is the atoning sacrifice for our sins, and not only for ours but also for the sins of the whole world.

STUFF TO KNOW Do you agree with that first zinger—verse 1:8—not to mention the second, in 1:10? Why or why not?

SIDELIGHT Lots of us are clueless as to how we measure up to God's total goodness. Like a high school basketball hotshot, you might figure you can play center in the NBA—until you stand next to a guy just shy of eight feet tall. Face it: When you become a Christian, God starts remaking you. But you're far from immediately perfect. This side of heaven, in fact, you won't ever be totally unflawed. Doubt that? See how you measure up against the lists of right and wrong in Ephesians 4:25–5:4 or Galatians 5:19–21.

Suppose you just did something wrong. When you've fallen down, God could wag a finger at you—and then whack you. But he chooses to help you up. So what does God want *you* to do (verse 1:9)?

DA'SCOOP To "confess" literally means "to say the same thing." It's admitting that your sin is sin—and as wrong as God says it is.

What does God promise to do when you admit your sins to him (verse 1:9)?

It can't get any more obvious than this: Why is John writing? What if things aren't going so swell (verse 2:1)?

SIDELIGHT Even after that loud challenge to get sin out of your life, this Bible Chunk sends you a roaring reminder of God's grace: Because of Jesus, you can grab hold of forgiveness! Here's the best news: When God makes that promise to forgive, it's un-breakable. So when you confess your sins to him, your sins are *gone*. Like Psalm 103:12 says, "He has taken our sins away from us as far as the east is from west" (NCV).

BIG QUESTIONS You're *reconciled* to God. You're being *remade* by him. God also wants you to be *responsive* to him—to fess up after you mess up, and then keep pressing close to him. How well are you doing at that?

So what do you do *now* when you realize you've done something wrong?

What would you like to change about the *next* time you biff?

Think of the Christians you know. Got any friends who are respon-sive to God—swift to admit they're wrong, quick to get back up when they've fallen down?

Do you suppose you're supposed to drop friends who aren't perfect? Explain.

DEEP THOT If you want friends really worth sticking to, start by looking for the *reconciled*—the ones who know God. Then look for those who are being *remade*—the ones who are growing. And if you find a friend who's *responsive* to God—well, that's the best kind of friend you could ever find. Glue yourself to that godly friend.

STICKY STUFF Remember 1 John 1:8–9. You're bound to need it sometime soon.

ACT ON IT Some Christians who mess up can't accept God's forgiveness when they fess up. Or they fess up and can't stop messing up. If that's you, find a wise older Christian to talk to.

DIG ON Check Psalm 103:8–12 to see where God chucks your sins when you confess them to him.

(15.) Suck It Up
(You need Christian friends to survive)

You've collected an impressive assortment of Christian friends who are *reconciled, undergoing a remake*, and *responsive to God*. But you've decided they're sometimes a hassle. You're not sure how to handle them—until you hear about Chillin' Chambers. "Just insert each of your Christian friends in one of our hermetically sealable pods." The salesguy smiles. "Suck out all the air, then set the chamber on deep freeze. Your friends are now completely maintenance-free—and you can forget about them ever hassling you again about things like right and wrong. Of course, we can't guarantee how long it will take them to warm up to you, should you need them in an emergency."

BRAIN DRAIN What are your chances of keeping your faith aflame if you put your Christian friends on ice?

FLASHBACK Look at it this way: Put your friends in a spiritual deep freeze, and the *best* you can hope for is never having the hot faith God wants for you. This next Bible Chunk comes a few chapters before that command in Hebrews 10:25 to "not give up meeting together" and to "encourage one another." That Bible Chunk tells you *what* to do. This one tells you *why*.

BIBLE CHUNK Read Hebrews 3:12–19 (NLT)

> (12) Be careful then, dear friends. Make sure that your own hearts are not evil and unbelieving, turning you away from the living God. (13) You

must warn each other every day, as long as it is called "today," so that none of you will be deceived by sin and hardened against God. (14) For if we are faithful to the end, trusting God just as firmly as when we first believed, we will share in all that belongs to Christ. (15) But never forget the warning:

> "Today you must listen to his voice.
> Don't harden your hearts against him
> as Israel did when they rebelled."

(16) And who were those people who rebelled against God, even though they heard his voice? Weren't they the ones Moses led out of Egypt? (17) And who made God angry for forty years? Wasn't it the people who sinned, whose bodies fell in the wilderness? (18) And to whom was God speaking when he vowed that they would never enter his place of rest? He was speaking to those who disobeyed him. (19) So we see that they were not allowed to enter his rest because of their unbelief.

STUFF TO KNOW What does the writer of Hebrews worry will happen to his readers (verses 12–13)?

What solution does he command? What are you and your Christian friends supposed to do for each other (verse 13)?

INSIGHT Christians can be duped into thinking sin looks good and God looks bad. The remedy? Daily doses of reality dropped kindly on you by other Christians—both warning and encouragement.

SIDELIGHT Warnings aren't always ugly, and encouraging others isn't just gooshy feelings. *Try reminding your friends who God is:* He never makes dumb rules (Psalm 19:7–9). He's good and loving in everything he does (Psalm 145:17). *Try reminding your friends what's right:* obeying parents (Colossians 3:20), slamming a lid on gossip (James 1:26), speaking with purity about the opposite sex (Ephesians 5:3–4), plus lots of other things you know are good.

What are you supposed to do if you "hear God's voice" (verse 15)?

INSIGHT That last line about Israel's rebellion unlocks the rest of this Bible Chunk. Back toward the beginning of the Old Testament, God saved his people from slavery in Egypt. They had been wowed by God's awesome, miraculous acts. They heard his voice. They knew his commands. Their problem? They still refused to trust God's power and care.

Blunt stuff: What consequence did they face (verse 19)?

INSIGHT When those Old Testament folks refused to obey God, they didn't stop being his people. But they didn't "enter his rest," get to live in and enjoy the incredible land he'd promised them. Instead, they spent the next forty years wandering in a desert wasteland. The same point still applies: When you don't trust and obey God, you never know what peace and good stuff from God you miss out on.

BIG QUESTIONS What do you want your Christian friends to do—or not do—to help you stay obedient to God?

How would you rattle the head of a friend who thinks sin looks attractive?

Do you buy the idea that your spiritual well-being really depends on your Christian friends? Why or why not?

DEEP THOT The secret to hanging tight with God is obeying his voice as soon as you hear it—learning his Word, the Bible, and letting him zing it home to your life. And the secret to obeying God's voice is having a bunch of friends to help you hear it. So listen up to God—together—or you'll miss God's best.

STICKY STUFF Memorize Hebrews 3:12–13 with a friend.

ACT ON IT Pray for the faith of one or two of your Christian friends. Then talk about never letting each other be deceived by sin or hardened against God.

DIG ON Check out Hebrews 4 to see how the author of Hebrews applied this point to Christians.

Talk About It • 3

EMPATHIZE: What's going on in your life?
ENCOURAGE: How are you doing with Jesus?
EQUIP: What one truth will you take home today?

- How much fun would it be to be best friends with a dead guy? How is that like having a best friend who doesn't know God? (Study 11)
- When have you felt encouraged—tapped into God—from hanging tight with Christian friends? (Study 11)
- Do you feel like you are God's friend? What makes you sure—or not sure? (Study 12)
- Is it snobbish—or worse—to make it your aim to find Christian friends? Why or why not? (Study 12)
- What does it mean to be remade by God? (Study 13)
- Suppose you have a friend who knows Christ but doesn't ever think about growing spiritually—getting remade in how he acts toward himself, others, or God. Would you pick that person as a really close friend? Why or why not? (Study 13)
- How quick are you to admit it when you're wrong? Why is that important? (Study 14)
- What's it mean to be responsive to God? What does that have to do with picking your closest friends? (Study 14)
- What are your chances of keeping your faith aflame if you put your Christian friends on ice? (Study 15)
- What do you want your Christian friends to do—or not do—to help you stay obedient to God? (Study 15)
- How would you rattle the head of a friend who thinks sin looks attractive? (Study 15)

PART 4

WHEN GOOD FRIENDS GO BAD

16. No Wuss-out
(Doing good to evildoers)

You live in a thump-or-be-thumped world: You get poked in the nose—you're supposed to punch back. You get put down—and you unleash a verbal bazooka. You get hit—you're expected to hit back harder. But on days when it gets tough to tell your friends from your enemies, Jesus shows you a better way. In this Bible Chunk you spot him hanging on the cross. It looks like he's losing the battle. Actually, he's winning the war.

BRAIN DRAIN How do you react when people trash you?

FLASHBACK Jesus knows what it's like to be on the receiving end of abuse. Consider these ugly things that happened to him on the way to his crucifixion: His family ripped on him—for a while, anyway (John 7:5). His religious opponents schemed to murder him (Matthew 26:4). A friend sold him out (Matthew 26:49). Soldiers stripped him naked. They twisted a crown of thorns and forced it onto his skull. Over and over, they struck him on the head with a staff (Matthew 27:26–30). And after that? They nailed him by his hands and feet to a cross.

BIBLE CHUNK Read Luke 23:32–49

(32) Two other men, both criminals, were also led out with him to be executed. (33) When they came to the place called the Skull, there they crucified him, along with the criminals—one on his right, the other on his

left. (34) Jesus said, "Father, forgive them, for they do not know what they are doing." And they divided up his clothes by casting lots.

(35) The people stood watching, and the rulers even sneered at him. They said, "He saved others; let him save himself if he is the Christ of God, the Chosen One."

(36) The soldiers also came up and mocked him. They offered him wine vinegar (37) and said, "If you are the king of the Jews, save yourself."

(38) There was a written notice above him, which read: THIS IS THE KING OF THE JEWS.

(39) One of the criminals who hung there hurled insults at him: "Aren't you the Christ? Save yourself and us!"

(40) But the other criminal rebuked him. "Don't you fear God," he said, "since you are under the same sentence? (41) We are punished justly, for we are getting what our deeds deserve. But this man has done nothing wrong."

(42) Then he said, "Jesus, remember me when you come into your kingdom."

(43) Jesus answered him, "I tell you the truth, today you will be with me in paradise."

(44) It was now about the sixth hour, and darkness came over the whole land until the ninth hour, (45) for the sun stopped shining. And the curtain of the temple was torn in two. (46) Jesus called out with a loud voice, "Father, into your hands I commit my spirit." When he had said this, he breathed his last.

(47) The centurion, seeing what had happened, praised God and said, "Surely this was a righteous man." (48) When all the people who had gathered to witness this sight saw what took place, they beat their breasts and went away. (49) But all those who knew him, including the women who had followed him from Galilee, stood at a distance, watching these things.

STUFF TO KNOW What cruel things do people do to Jesus in this scene at the cross? Make a list from verses 34–39.

So what did Jesus do to deserve all this suffering (verses 41, 47–48)?

SIDELIGHT If Jesus didn't deserve death—if he was utterly sinless (Hebrews 4:15)—how did he end up on the cross? Did he just wuss out and let himself be killed? Not that long before, Jesus had evaded enemies aiming to do him in (Matthew 12:14–15). At the cross, he could have called an army of angels to save him— yet he didn't (Matthew 26:53). He embraced the cross (Hebrews 12:2) because he knew his death was the only way he could bring human beings back to God: As the totally innocent Son of God, he "carried our sins in his body on the cross so we would stop living for sin and start living for what is right. And you are healed because of his wounds" (1 Peter 2:24 NCV).

You'd think Jesus would blast his killers with a lightning bolt. What's he do instead (verse 34)?

BIG QUESTIONS If you have a choice between praying for an enemy or punching his lights out, which do you choose?

Why was Jesus able to hack it when people hurt him?

SIDELIGHT Two answers from other Bible Chunks: Reason one: Jesus entrusted himself to him who judges justly (1 Peter 1:23–24). In other words, he knew he was innocent—more importantly, so did his heavenly Father. Reason two: He knew by going to the cross he was being absolutely obedient to his Father's will (Philippians 2:8).

What good does it do you to know God is watching out for you when you bang heads or get beat up?

DEEP THOT The Bible presents what Jesus did on the cross as nothing less than an example for you to follow: "Christ suffered for you, leaving you an example, that you should follow in his steps. . . . When they hurled their insults at him, he did not retaliate; when he suffered, he made no threats" (1 Peter 2:21, 23). When you hand someone love instead of hatred, your world sees Jesus in you.

STICKY STUFF Next time you're getting kicked, remember Jesus' words from the cross: Luke 23:34.

ACT ON IT Jesus doesn't expect you to be stupid. If you or a friend is getting hit at home or bullied at school, run for help to an adult you trust.

DIG ON Read Romans 12:17–21 for the straight scoop on how to heap burning coals on your enemies' heads.

17 You've Got a Pile of Friends—*Somewhere*
(Conquering loneliness)

Jamie sits quietly at Bible study, head in hands and stomach in a knot. Her youth pastor is really wise—and way better than tolerable to listen to. But between the spit wads that keep thonking her forehead when she looks up and the couple making face-sucking noises behind her, it's ridiculous trying to focus. She feels awful that no one else takes the study seriously—not just for her or for her youth pastor, but for them. *Doesn't anyone else feel like I do?* she wonders.

BRAIN DRAIN How do you stay sane when life—especially wanting to do the right thing—leaves you feeling alone?

FLASHBACK It happens: The Christian life that's supposed to bequeath you many merry friendships brings you . . . well, squat. Don't fret: God gives you two ways to solve the ghastly aloneness that sooner or later strikes all who follow God. The first is to get close to him—lots more on that in section five. The second is to grab hold of his people. And as you'll see in this Bible Chunk, if you don't see any of God's people around, you get to tell him straight-up. Elijah—a prophet, one of God's most major spokespersons of all time—totals up his friends and gets zilch. Hunted by the armies of a wicked queen, Elijah hikes for forty days and crawls into a cave. Here's what he says to God:

BIBLE CHUNK Read 1 Kings 19:9–18

(9) There he [Elijah] went into a cave and spent the night.

And the word of the Lord came to him: "What are you doing here, Elijah?"

(10) He replied, "I have been very zealous for the Lord God Almighty. The Israelites have rejected your covenant, broken down your altars, and put your prophets to death with the sword. I am the only one left, and now they are trying to kill me too."

(11) The Lord said, "Go out and stand on the mountain in the presence of the Lord, for the Lord is about to pass by."

Then a great and powerful wind tore the mountains apart and shattered the rocks before the Lord, but the Lord was not in the wind. After the wind there was an earthquake, but the Lord was not in the earthquake. (12) After the earthquake came a fire, but the Lord was not in the fire. And after the fire came a gentle whisper. (13) When Elijah heard it, he pulled his cloak over his face and went out and stood at the mouth of the cave.

Then a voice said to him, "What are you doing here, Elijah?"

(14) He replied, "I have been very zealous for the Lord God Almighty. The Israelites have rejected your covenant, broken down your altars, and put your prophets to death with the sword. I am the only one left, and now they are trying to kill me too."

(15) The Lord said to him, "Go back the way you came, and go to the Desert of Damascus. When you get there, anoint Hazael king over Aram. (16) Also, anoint Jehu son of Nimshi king over Israel, and anoint Elisha son of Shaphat from Abel Meholah to succeed you as prophet. (17) Jehu will put to death any who escape the sword of Hazael, and Elisha will put to death any who escape the sword of Jehu. (18) Yet I reserve seven thousand in Israel—all whose knees have not bowed down to Baal and all whose mouths have not kissed him."

STUFF TO KNOW What's Elijah so down about (verse 10)?

SIDELIGHT Only a month had passed since Elijah stood on Mt. Carmel, one man against 450 prophets of the fake god Baal. At Elijah's request, God flung fire from heaven to torch a sacrifice— stone altar and all (1 Kings 18:19–40). Baal lost. God won. But right before this Bible Chunk, Elijah tells God he'd be happier dead. How

come? Elijah thinks he's the one-and-only true believer in God in a country packed with pagans.

Does God sound like he's ready to spew anger at Elijah for how he feels? (Think about how God talks to Elijah through this whole Bible Chunk. . . .)

God tells Elijah to take a short hike. What happens? What's the shake, rattle, and roll supposed to prove (verses 11–13)?

INSIGHT Rocks shatter. The earth shakes. The mountain burns. God, however, doesn't show up in any of those spectacular demonstrations of power. He instead comes to Elijah in calmness—"a gentle whisper," or what the King James Version of the Bible famously calls a "still small voice." God is present to soothe Elijah, not scream at him.

God's whisper means "Trust me!" But Elijah grabs his chance to moan some more. Then what does God promise Elijah (verses 15–18)?

INSIGHT Get this: Instead of packing Elijah off to retirement at a palm-lined oasis, God sends him *back to where he came from.* But God also radically rearranges his situation. Elijah is to install a new king in Aram, a nation constantly at war with Israel. He gets to declare a new king over Israel—to replace the wicked queen who's hunting him. Elijah gets Elisha—a serious spiritual partner. And he finds out he has 7,000 other faithful-to-God friends he didn't even know about.

BIG QUESTIONS When has being a Christian made you more lonely—not less?

What do you *expect* God to do about loneliness? What do you believe he *can* do about that? What are you *willing* to ask him for?

DEEP THOT Think about it: God told Elijah he had some friends for him—and then he made Elijah *go get them*. Elijah's crisis of loneliness had more to do with his lack of faith in God than with his apparent lack of friends.

ACT ON IT Ask God for help when you feel lonely. And if you don't feel lonely, ask God to help you meet the needs of someone who does.

STICKY STUFF First Kings 19:18 says that when you're down and troubled, and you need a helping hand—you've got a friend.

DIG ON Flip to Hebrews 13:5, where God promises to never leave you.

18. The Rules
(God's top ten rules for relationships)

"She's lying," Bekka wails. "Mary is telling everyone that I stole her boyfriend. I had nothing to do with them breaking up. He hates her guts—he told me. And we're not even going out—yet. I know she's annoyed that I borrowed her math book out of her locker—and some money from her purse—and that I didn't put them back. But those are no big deal. What's she so wound up about?"

BRAIN DRAIN Where do you head for advice when your relationships go freakazoid?

FLASHBACK Face it: You can do better than deciding who's right and who's wrong based on consulting your feelings— or by playing favorites—or by hurling baseball bats. You want to look to the Bible for one-of-a-kind wisdom. All Scripture, says 2 Timothy 3:15, "is useful to teach us what is true and to make us realize what is wrong in our lives. It straightens us out and teaches us to do what is right" (NLT). God's Word is the referee you need when enemies hammer you—or when good friends go bad. This next chunk spells out God's top ten rules for relationships—his ultra-important Ten Commandments.

BIBLE CHUNK Read Exodus 20:1–8, 12–17

(1) And God spoke all these words:
(2) "I am the Lord your God, who brought you out of Egypt, out of the land of slavery.

(3) "You shall have no other gods before me.

(4) "You shall not make for yourself an idol in the form of anything in heaven above or on the earth beneath or in the waters below. (5) You shall not bow down to them or worship them; for I, the Lord your God, am a jealous God, punishing the children for the sin of the fathers to the third and fourth generation of those who hate me, (6) but showing love to a thousand generations of those who love me and keep my commandments.

(7) "You shall not misuse the name of the Lord your God, for the Lord will not hold anyone guiltless who misuses his name.

(8) "Remember the Sabbath day by keeping it holy. . . .

(12) "Honor your father and your mother, so that you may live long in the land the Lord your God is giving you.

(13) "You shall not murder.

(14) "You shall not commit adultery.

(15) "You shall not steal.

(16) "You shall not give false testimony against your neighbor.

(17) "You shall not covet your neighbor's house. You shall not covet your neighbor's wife, or his manservant or maidservant, his ox or donkey, or anything that belongs to your neighbor."

STUFF TO KNOW Hmm . . . so who makes the rules (verse 1)? How come (verse 2)?

SIDELIGHT God could have claimed the right to make rules based on the fact that he made humankind—as in you-make-it, you-da-master-of-it. Instead, he reminds his Old Testament people that he yanked them out of slavery—he saved them. Know what? Jesus has the same claim on you. Remember Titus 2:14? He "gave himself for us to redeem us from all wickedness and to purify for himself a people that are his very own, eager to do what is good." That "redeem" thing he did literally means he "bought back" humanity from sin's grasp. He paid for you. So he owns you.

What's rule number one (verse 3)?

INSIGHT Rules for getting along with God occupy the first four slots in God's top-ten list of right and wrong. That's not conceit. It's admitting that God is Ultimate Power, Ultimate Wisdom, and Ultimate Love. He's got what it takes to run your life—and run it right.

Blunt news: How long do the effects of wandering from God last (verse 5)? Better news: How about the rewards for loving God (verse 6)?

Next come six commands for getting along with your peers and other people. Explain 'em in your own words:

- Verse 12:

- Verse 13:

- Verse 14:

- Verse 15:

- Verse 16:

- Verse 17:

DA'SCOOP To *honor* means both to respect and to prize highly. *Murder* is premeditated killing, including suicide.

Adultery covers sex outside of marriage. *Stealing* applies to solid stuff and to people. *False testimony* is lying of any kind. And *coveting* is longing for someone else's stuff—computers, cars, wardrobe, looks, significant others . . . you get the idea.

BIG QUESTIONS Which of those commands is toughest for you to follow? Why?

Think of a friendship that's not so hot right now. Get honest: Are *you* breaking any of these big-time relationship rules?

INSIGHT You're probably not planning on killing anyone—this week, anyway. Jesus, though, keeps you from getting too self-righteous. Calling someone a fool, he says, is as bad as murder (Matthew 5:22). And looking at a woman lustfully counts as adultery (Matthew 5:27–28). Ponder this: God's commands have as much to do with attitudes as with actions.

DEEP THOT God's Ten Commandments don't leave any doubt about right and wrong. And those are just starters. God's entire Word is a measuring stick for your relationships. It tells you for sure when you're being slammed. And it tells you too when you're the source of the problem.

ACT ON IT Sit down with a Christian friend you're having a hard time with. Admit what you've been doing wrong.

STICKY STUFF Use Exodus 20:1–3 to remind yourself who makes the rules.

DIG ON Dig through Colossians 3:5–17 for more relationship rules.

(19) Help, Please!
(Four steps for getting along)

"I'm doomed," Erik groans. "I'm sick of Blake copying my work. How can the teacher not notice him? A bunch of people say I should tell on him—that sounds like a suggestion my mother would make. If I tell the teacher, I'll probably get in trouble too. I should know. The same thing happened to me in science once, and the teacher punished us both. Besides that, I don't want to look like a wuss."

BRAIN DRAIN Suppose you'd really like to screech to a stop someone else's nasty actions. What should you do?

FLASHBACK Lots of people figure Christianity is a religion for people who like to get rolled over. Actually, everything that Jesus teaches implies you should fight for what's right. He even outlines what to do when someone wrongs you. Sure, some hurts you can overlook. But when you can't let it slide—it's too big, it bothers you too much, or it harms someone you're obligated to protect—try these wise insights from Jesus. You can think of this short and sassy Bible Chunk, in fact, as *God's Four Steps to Getting Along*. . . .

BIBLE CHUNK Read Matthew 18:15–17

(15) "If your brother sins against you, go and show him his fault, just between the two of you. If he listens to you, you have won your brother over. (16) But if he will not listen, take one or two others along, so that

'every matter may be established by the testimony of two or three witnesses.' (17) If he refuses to listen to them, tell it to the church; and if he refuses to listen even to the church, treat him as you would a pagan or a tax collector."

STUFF TO KNOW Someone wrongs you. What's your first step? Tar and super glue (verse 15)?

INSIGHT Oooo . . . scary step. You're actually supposed to tell someone you're ticked to their face? And in private? Yep. And screaming at someone doesn't count. You're to speak the truth *with love* (Ephesians 4:15)—that is, with an aim not of proving your rightness but repairing the relationship.

What's the whopper payoff if your opponent listens to you (verse 15)?

You try that. Nothing happens. What's step two (verse 16)?

INSIGHT Jesus' goal isn't for you and your chums to gang up on a wrongdoer, but to get at the facts. That's what it means for "every matter" to be "established by the testimony of two or three witnesses" (Deuteronomy 19:15).

Once again, you try that. Your opponent continues in his or her obnoxiousness. What comes next (front half of verse 17)?

INSIGHT Spot a principle—or a principal? That verse applies to every part of your life. Once you have tried to solve a problem yourself—and with another observer—your next step is to appeal to an authority. Get this: If you're not getting the help you need, that higher-up almost always has a higher-up. But things are getting serious. Think hard: Do you want to drag an adult into the situation? Is the problem big enough? What might it cost you?

And finally—you're ready to explode. You've done all that. Nothing happens. What now (back half of verse 17)?

INSIGHT Those serious words mean "have nothing to do with him!" The Bible isn't stupid. You won't win over everyone. That's reality. Like Romans 12:18 says, "If it is possible, as far as it depends on you, live at peace with everyone." Sometimes you need to take a break from the friendship—or get out of a situation totally.

BIG QUESTIONS Can you think of a time you took steps like that to fix things with a friend—whether or not you knew about Matthew 18? How did it help? What was hard?

Let's sum up those four steps in everyday language. Jesus says to

- Step 1: Talk in private.
- Step 2: Bring a witness.
- Step 3: Appeal to an authority.
- Step 4: Take a break from the relationship.

So are those four steps a handy idea? Why or why not?

What's tough about taking that first step?

INSIGHT Quiz time: What ugly labels do you have for people who rocket past these steps? People who won't talk to you first are *gossips* or *backbiters*. Peers who run straight to a parent or a teacher are *tattletales* or *bigmouths* or *blabs*. And anyone who immediately cuts you off is—*names too nasty to mention*. You hate it when people do those things. Jesus knows your world.

What situations in your life need solving? How are you going to use this process to help?

DEEP THOT Ponder this way-old wisdom: " 'You must not hate your fellow citizen in your heart. If your neighbor does something wrong, tell him about it, or you will be partly to blame. Forget about the wrong things people do to you, and do not try to get even. Love your neighbor as you love yourself. I am the Lord' " (Leviticus 19:17–18 NCV).

ACT ON IT Talk with a mature Christian about how you can use this process to untangle some mess in your life.

STICKY STUFF Mull Matthew 18:15 over until it makes sense to you.

DIG ON Don't miss 1 Peter 4:8. "Love covers a multitude of sins," by the way, doesn't mean "sweep sins under the rug." It means that love doesn't blab about the faults of others.

(20.) Happy Feet
(Keeping on when evil wins)

With each passing year, Natalie has watched one friend after another walk away from God. Drinking, drugs, out-of-control guy-girl "stuff"—you name it, her friends have done it. But whenever Natalie thinks about how God has taken care of her—and given her a handful of good friends who stick close to him—she knows she wants nothing more than to follow God.

BRAIN DRAIN Have you ever thought that following God is stupid? What got you smart again?

FLASHBACK This Bible Chunk gives you all but the last few words of the last book of the Old Testament. God's people are taking it on the chin—and they're not smiling. They'd forgotten a huge word of comfort from way back in Israel's history: "The Lord searches all the earth for people who have given themselves completely to him. He wants to make them strong" (2 Chronicles 16:9 NCV). God knows who's hanging tight to him. And guess what? He also knows who's not.

BIBLE CHUNK Read Malachi 3:13–4:3

(3:13) "You have said harsh things against me," says the Lord.
"Yet you ask, 'What have we said against you?'
(3:14) "You have said, 'It is futile to serve God. What did we gain by carrying out his requirements and going about like mourners before the Lord Almighty? (3:15) But now we call the arrogant blessed. Certainly the evildoers prosper, and even those who challenge God escape.' "

(3:16) Then those who feared the Lord talked with each other, and the Lord listened and heard. A scroll of remembrance was written in his presence concerning those who feared the Lord and honored his name.

(3:17) "They will be mine," says the Lord Almighty, "in the day when I make up my treasured possession. I will spare them, just as in compassion a man spares his son who serves him. (3:18) And you will again see the distinction between the righteous and the wicked, between those who serve God and those who do not.

(4:1) "Surely the day is coming; it will burn like a furnace. All the arrogant and every evildoer will be stubble, and that day that is coming will set them on fire," says the Lord Almighty. "Not a root or a branch will be left to them. (4:2) But for you who revere my name, the sun of righteousness will rise with healing in its wings. And you will go out and leap like calves released from the stall. (4:3) Then you will trample down the wicked; they will be ashes under the soles of your feet on the day when I do these things," says the Lord Almighty.

STUFF TO KNOW According to the folks at the start
of this Bible Chunk, how great is it to serve God—or not (verse 3:14)? Why (verse 3:15)?

God aims those sharp words of correction at all of Israel. But apparently not everyone is messed up in how they think about God and his commands. What would you guess the folks in 3:16 are gabbing about? What does God do with the info he overhears (verse 3:16)?

SIDELIGHT God isn't Santa Claus—making his list and
checking it twice. But the idea of him keeping a book of people who belong to him also appears in Hebrews 12:23 and Revelation 21:27, among other places.

God says people fall into two groups—the righteous and the wicked. How can you tell who's who (verse 3:18)?

What destiny does God have planned for evildoers (verse 4:1)?

DA'SCOOP *The day*—often called "the Day of the Lord" in the Old Testament—is actually an *event*. It's the moment in the future when God will judge Israel and the world (like in Obadiah 1:15). The New Testament adds that *the day* is the time of Christ's return (2 Thessalonians 2:2; 2 Peter 3:10).

What does God have in store for the good guys and gals while that tough stuff is happening (verse 4:2)?

INSIGHT That "sun of righteousness" that will "rise with healing in its wings" sounds like Jesus, and some Bibles capitalize the word "Sun" to show that. That phrase for sure means that God's people will get spiritual insight and healing. And they'll get happy feet—like cow babies let loose from the stall.

BIG QUESTION How bad do you spew when life goes good for bad people?

What keeps you doing right when doing wrong would get you ahead?

So does it sound like God gives *you* the job of dishing out disastrous punishment to bad folks?

SIDELIGHT The end of this Bible Chunk talks about, well, the end of time. For now, chew on this choice bit from the Bible: "Dear friends, never avenge yourselves. Leave that to God. For it is written, 'I will take vengeance; I will repay those who deserve it,' says the Lord" (Romans 12:19 NLT). Punishment of evildoers is certain. But it won't come from you.

Does God really notice when you stick close to him? Do you think doing right will do you any good? How? When?

DEEP THOT Trust this fact: God doesn't always make you wait until the end of the world to experience his rewards. Like Galatians 6:9 says: "So don't get tired of doing what is good. Don't get discouraged and give up, for we will reap a harvest of blessing at the appropriate time" (NLT).

ACT ON IT Make a list of the things that make it hard for you to keep following God. Talk through your list with a mature Christian.

STICKY STUFF Malachi 4:2 means you'd better sign up for bovine dancing lessons.

DIG ON Take a look at Psalm 73 when you feel foolish for following God.

Talk About It • 4

EMPATHIZE: What's going on in your life?
ENCOURAGE: How are you doing with Jesus?
EQUIP: What one truth will you take home today?

- How do you react when people trash you? (Study 16)
- If you have a choice between praying for an enemy or punching his lights out, which do you choose? (Study 16)
- Why was Jesus able to hack it when people hurt him? (Study 16)
- How do you stay sane when life—especially wanting to do the right thing—leaves you feeling alone? (Study 17)
- When has being a Christian made you more lonely—not less? (Study 17)
- What do you *expect* God to do about loneliness? What do you believe he *can* do about that? What are you *willing* to ask him for? (Study 17)
- Where do you head for advice when your relationships get weird? How do you decide who's right—and who's wrong? (Study 18)
- Think of a friendship that's not so hot right now. Are you breaking any of God's big-time relationship rules? (Study 18)
- Suppose you'd like to stop someone else's nasty actions. What should you do? (Study 19)
- What are the four steps Jesus talked about for solving relationship ugliness? (Study 19)
- Have you ever thought that following God is stupid? What got you smart again? (Study 20)
- What keeps you doing right when doing wrong would get you ahead? (Study 20)
- Does God give you the job of dishing out punishments to bad folks? (Study 20)

PART 5

YOUR
ULTIMATE
BEST
FRIEND

㉑ Hang Tight
(Friends can let you down)

You'd like to think that friends don't let friends go through life alone. But sometimes you *drift*—you and a buddy head so far in different directions that your one-time friend looks like a tiny stick figure in your rearview mirror. Other times a friend takes a flying leap—into *destruction*. Or a friend moves away—and *distance* yanks you apart. And—whether you've pondered this or not—someday you'll face a friend's *death*. And whenever you're left alone, part of you withers.

BRAIN DRAIN When has a friend totally left you down and out?

FLASHBACK Just before the unhappy friend-dumping-friend account you'll read about in this Bible Chunk, a "mob armed with swords and clubs" arrests Jesus in a garden and takes him to the head priest (Mark 14:54). As Jesus is dragged away, his disciple Peter follows at a distance, right into the courtyard where Jesus' trial takes place. And get this: While Jesus gets mocked, beaten, and spit on, Peter warms his backside by the guards' fire (Mark 14:63, 65)! Yep—that's the friend who swore he would gladly die with Jesus. It's also the friend Jesus had predicted would disown him three times before a rooster crowed twice (Mark 14:31). As Peter watches Jesus from the shadows, watch what Peter does. . . .

BIBLE CHUNK Read Mark 14:66–72

(66) While Peter was below in the courtyard, one of the servant girls of the high priest came by. (67) When she saw Peter warming himself, she looked closely at him.

"You also were with that Nazarene, Jesus," she said.

(68) But he denied it. "I don't know or understand what you're talking about," he said, and went out into the entryway.

(69) When the servant girl saw him there, she said again to those standing around, "This fellow is one of them." (70) Again he denied it.

After a little while, those standing near said to Peter, "Surely you are one of them, for you are a Galilean."

(71) He began to call down curses on himself, and he swore to them, "I don't know this man you're talking about."

(72) Immediately the rooster crowed the second time. Then Peter remembered the word Jesus had spoken to him: "Before the rooster crows twice you will disown me three times." And he broke down and wept.

STUFF TO KNOW Who's the first person to jump on Peter? What does she accuse him of (verse 67)?

Peter stands up for Jesus, right? What's he say (verse 68)?

INSIGHT Nothing against servant girls, but notice how this brawny grown guy is being bullied by an ankle-biter.

Who's the second person to accuse Peter (verse 69)?

INSIGHT Surprise! The little servant comes back for another bite. Peter had moved from warming himself by the fire to standing in an entry. And the servant girl had riled up a crowd to accuse Peter (verse 70).

Read it carefully: Who does Peter curse (verse 71)?

INSIGHT Peter isn't mad at himself. His curses are calling down God's wrath if he's lying—a big-time "cross my heart and hope to die, stick a needle in my eye"! Notice how Peter's denials are getting darker? The first two times Peter is confronted he says he isn't Jesus' follower. This time he denies knowing Jesus altogether.

What happens next (verse 72)?

SIDELIGHT That's one heart-stabbing cock-a-doodle-doo—the rooster crow that Jesus had prophesied in Mark 14:30. At that moment, reports Luke 22:61, Jesus stares straight at Peter. And then . . .

What does Peter suddenly remember? And what does he do (verse 72)?

BIG QUESTIONS Pretend you're Peter. How are you feeling right now?

Try this one: You're *Jesus.* Are you feeling yanked around by your friends—or what?

SIDELIGHT Shocking factoid: Jesus knew ahead of time that his good friend Peter would deny him. He let Peter be his friend anyway. And after Jesus rose from the dead, he brought Peter back into close friendship (John 21:15–19).

So how do you feel when your friends leave you hanging?

DEEP THOT When your friends dump you, Jesus understands. When you desert a friend, he understands. Even when you fall down in your friendship with him, he understands. Look—he understands it *all*, because he's been there.

ACT ON IT Who have *you* let down in the last few days? Go straighten it out.

STICKY STUFF Let the words of Mark 14:72 sink into your heart.

DIG ON Read John 21:15–19, where Jesus lets Peter know he still loves him—and vice versa.

22. You'll Survive
(God is your totally faithful friend)

When your social studies teacher announces a unit on "human societies and their organization," you nudge the girl next to you and ask her to wake you up in a few weeks. When your teacher trots your class off to a retreat on a remote island, you figure you're in for some fun. But when he says you'll have to scarf bugs to survive—and that all get to vote unpopular people off the island—you wonder how you'll do. And when you're the first person your classmates kick out of your island society, you crawl off and cry.

BRAIN DRAIN Who do you turn to when your enemies jump you—and your friends dump you?

FLASHBACK Back in the Old Testament, a guy named David was tough enough to survive some of life's harshest attacks. As a teenage shepherd he killed lions and bears trying to maul his sheep (1 Samuel 17:36). As a young guy he dodged spears hurled by an insane king (1 Samuel 18:10–11). And as an adult he became a fearsome warrior and king (1 Samuel 18:7). But when the whole world ganged up on him, he didn't depend on his own smarts to survive. He relied on God.

BIBLE CHUNK Read Psalm 27

(1) The Lord is my light and my salvation—
   whom shall I fear?
   The Lord is the stronghold of my life—

of whom shall I be afraid?
(2) When evil men advance against me
     to devour my flesh,
     when my enemies and my foes attack me,
     they will stumble and fall.
(3) Though an army besiege me,
     my heart will not fear;
     though war break out against me,
     even then will I be confident.
(4) One thing I ask of the Lord,
     this is what I seek:
     that I may dwell in the house of the Lord
     all the days of my life,
     to gaze upon the beauty of the Lord
     and to seek him in his temple.
(5) For in the day of trouble
     he will keep me safe in his dwelling;
     he will hide me in the shelter of his tabernacle
     and set me high upon a rock.
(6) Then my head will be exalted
     above the enemies who surround me;
     at his tabernacle will I sacrifice with shouts of joy;
     I will sing and make music to the Lord.
(7) Hear my voice when I call, O Lord;
     be merciful to me and answer me.
(8) My heart says of you, "Seek his face!"
     Your face, Lord, I will seek.
(9) Do not hide your face from me,
     do not turn your servant away in anger;
     you have been my helper.
     Do not reject me or forsake me,
     O God my Savior.
(10) Though my father and mother forsake me,
     the Lord will receive me.*
(11) Teach me your way, O Lord;
     lead me in a straight path
     because of my oppressors.
(12) Do not turn me over to the desire of my foes,
     for false witnesses rise up against me,
     breathing out violence.
(13) I am still confident of this:
     I will see the goodness of the Lord
     in the land of the living.
(14) Wait for the Lord;
     be strong and take heart
     and wait for the Lord.

STUFF TO KNOW You've got God on your side.
What do you have to be afraid of (verse 1)?

What kind of attacks does David face (verse 2)? In the midst of those major troubles, what's his top-of-the-list request for God (verse 4)?

Don't you think David should be begging God for bombs and bazookas? Why does he want God (verses 5–6)?

INSIGHT Oddly enough, David trusts God to keep him safe in the *tabernacle*—the tent where Israel worshiped God before the temple was built. He didn't find safety in a fort. He fled to God's presence.

When does David expect God's help to show up (verse 13)? What's he going to do in the meantime (verse 14)?

BIG QUESTIONS How does God figure into your plans when friends let you down?

Peek back at that Bible Chunk. What's the *first* thing to ask God for when you feel friendless? How could that help you?

What are some other kinds of help you can ask God for? What are you going to do while you wait?

DEEP THOT Even on days when you crawl away and curl up in a ball, you're never alone. God is your one friend who will never let you down.

ACT ON IT What do you need from God right now to help you survive and thrive in life? Talk to him about it.

STICKY STUFF Remember your number-one request: Psalm 22:4.

DIG ON Read more about the safety of sticking close to God in Psalm 84.

(23.) Hu Nose U?
(God knows you inside and out)

A few weeks after Sara's dad entered treatment for a hard-core drinking problem, he signed Sara up for a care group for teenage children of alcoholics. Meeting after meeting, Sara said nothing, scared to share how horrible life had been with an alcoholic dad. But as Sara studied each face and voice, she grew sure she was in a safe place. She exploded in tears. She unloaded her hurts. She finally had friends who understood the secret she'd tried her whole life to hide.

BRAIN DRAIN So what kinds of secrets are you afraid to tell even your best human friends?

FLASHBACK If you flip through the Psalms—the Bible's book of prayers—you peer inside the heart of David, that brave guy in your last Bible Chunk. Over and over you spot David unloading hurts (Psalm 6:3–6), keeping God up-to-date on his hassles (Psalm 22:6–18), confessing his sins (Psalm 51), and crying out for help (Psalm 5:1–3). David had figured out a huge fact: God knew him so totally that he never had to pretend he was something he wasn't. And there was nothing he ever had to hide from God.

BIBLE CHUNK Read Psalm 139:1–18

(1) O Lord, you have searched me
   and you know me.
(2) You know when I sit and when I rise;

you perceive my thoughts from afar.
(3) You discern my going out and my lying down;
  you are familiar with all my ways.
(4) Before a word is on my tongue
  you know it completely, O Lord.
(5) You hem me in—behind and before;
  you have laid your hand upon me.
(6) Such knowledge is too wonderful for me,
  too lofty for me to attain.
(7) Where can I go from your Spirit?
  Where can I flee from your presence?
(8) If I go up to the heavens, you are there;
  if I make my bed in the depths, you are there.
(9) If I rise on the wings of the dawn,
  if I settle on the far side of the sea,
(10) even there your hand will guide me,
  your right hand will hold me fast.
(11) If I say, "Surely the darkness will hide me
  and the light become night around me,"
(12) even the darkness will not be dark to you;
  the night will shine like the day,
  for darkness is as light to you.
(13) For you created my inmost being;
  you knit me together in my mother's womb.
(14) I praise you because I am fearfully and wonderfully made;
  your works are wonderful,
  I know that full well.
(15) My frame was not hidden from you
  when I was made in the secret place.
  When I was woven together in the depths of the earth,
(16) your eyes saw my unformed body.
  All the days ordained for me
  were written in your book
  before one of them came to be.
(17) How precious to me are your thoughts, O God!
  How vast is the sum of them!
(18) Were I to count them,
  they would outnumber the grains of sand.
  When I awake,
  I am still with you.

STUFF TO KNOW Make a list of all the things God knows about you (verses 1–6).

Does David think hiding from God is a hot idea? How come (verses 7–12)?

When God looks closely at David, what does he see (verses 13–18)?

BIG QUESTIONS Doesn't it make you a tad nervous to be scrutinized by the all-seeing eye of God? Why or why not?

SIDELIGHT There's no hiding from God. He knows every-thing about you—good, bad, or downright ugly. But here's a cool truth: Even when God sees you at your worst, he still loves you. Romans 5:8 says, in fact, that "God shows his great love for us in this way: Christ died for us while we were still sinners."

Is there anything you wish God didn't know about you? How come?

SIDELIGHT David had plenty of reasons to hide from God, but at the end of Psalm 139 he actually *invites* God to examine

his insides. "Search me, O God," he says, "and know my heart; test me and know my anxious thoughts. See if there is any offensive way in me, and lead me in the way everlasting" (Psalm 139:23–24). He saw God's total knowledge of him as the best way to under-stand himself—and for God to lead him into a better life.

How could it help you to be open with the God who knows you most?

DEEP THOT
God is even closer than your ultraclose human friends. He already knows everything you've ever thought, said, and done. And he sees the secrets you hide in your heart. If it's something you've done wrong, he'll help you. If it's a place where you hurt, he'll heal you. And if it's something you'd die with embarrassment for anyone else to find out, he'll guard your tender spots. God knows you most. And he likes you best.

STICKY STUFF
Psalm 139:1–2 says you've got a friend who knows you totally.

ACT ON IT
Think about some things you've never admit-ted to God—sins, hurts, stupid stuff—and have a chat with him. And don't forget that God doesn't expect you to face tough stuff alone—so have a chat with a trustworthy human friend too.

DIG ON
Read Psalm 51, David's most famous gut-wrenching episode of openness with God.

(24.) Fruit of the Loom
(Sticking tight to Jesus)

After thirteen years of hypersecret experiments in your basement laboratory, you've hatched a science fair project befitting your genius. Each morning while your peers sip OJ, you plug your index fingers into a socket—and via your Transfusional Electrical Interface, you're walloped with incredible energy. With a twenty-minute daily recharge you only need 2.3 hours of sleep per night, and your cravings for TV have dropped 47%. Your next goal? To download homework directly to your brain. Your ultimate goal? To conquer your faith—and achieve a high-bandwidth, always-on relationship with God.

BRAIN DRAIN How do you stay connected to God—the best being in the universe you could ever be best friends with?

FLASHBACK Cruel fact of life: Sometimes even the best of friends leave you lonely. But unlike human friends, God will never let you down. Hebrews 13:5–6 puts it like this: "God has said, 'I will never leave you; I will never forget you'" (NCV). But having God as your ultimate friend won't do you any good if you don't know how to live close to him. Living connected with God, by the way, doesn't involve sticking your finger in an electrical outlet. Then again, it's sorta the same.

BIBLE CHUNK Read John 15:5–14

(5) "I am the vine; you are the branches. If a man remains in me and I in him, he will bear much fruit; apart from me you can do nothing. (6) If

anyone does not remain in me, he is like a branch that is thrown away and withers; such branches are picked up, thrown into the fire and burned. (7) If you remain in me and my words remain in you, ask whatever you wish, and it will be given you. (8) This is to my Father's glory, that you bear much fruit, showing yourselves to be my disciples.

(9) "As the Father has loved me, so have I loved you. Now remain in my love. (10) If you obey my commands, you will remain in my love, just as I have obeyed my Father's commands and remain in his love. (11) I have told you this so that my joy may be in you and that your joy may be complete. (12) My command is this: Love each other as I have loved you. (13) Greater love has no one than this, that he lay down his life for his friends. (14) You are my friends if you do what I command."

STUFF TO KNOW Funky: What does Jesus call himself (verse 5)?

Think horticulturally. If you don't stick tight with Jesus, what will happen? What won't (verse 5)?

SIDELIGHT Fruit is big in the Bible. Fruit shows what a person is really like (Matthew 7:16). Failing to produce good fruit gets a plant chopped down (Matthew 7:19). And when you're connected to Jesus, you produce fruit like love, joy, peace, patience, kindness, goodness, faithfulness, gentleness, and self-control (Galatians 5:22–23).

What happens to a branch that doesn't bear fruit (verse 6)?

INSIGHT Maybe you don't know an artichoke from your armpit. Jesus gives a simple lesson in gardening: A branch only

bears fruit if it's connected to the vine. And if a branch doesn't bear fruit, something's drastically wrong.

DA'SCOOP That six-letter word *remain* is the big point of this whole Bible Chunk—and it means to *stay connected* to Jesus. The first part of this chunk (verses 5–8) says you do that by drawing life from him—getting nourishment from his Word, the Bible. The second part (verses 9–14) says you remain in Jesus by obeying him—living a life of love.

What happens when you remain in Jesus—and his teachings have taken hold of your heart (verse 7)?

SIDELIGHT That's no promise to answer your every whim. To have God's words means you will ask according to what *God* wants—the same condition for answered prayer described in 1 John 5:14: "And this is the boldness we have in God's presence: that if we ask God for anything that agrees with what he wants, he hears us" (NCV).

What happens when you obey God (verse 10)? Is the experience of sticking tight to Jesus supposed to be awful (verse 11)?

INSIGHT You don't earn God's love. But obeying God lets you enjoy it. It keeps you tight with your source of life. It's like having your head and heart plugged into God.

BIG QUESTIONS Do you ever feel far from God? What makes you feel that way?

When God feels far away, where do you suppose he's wandered off to?

INSIGHT Trick question. In case it's been a long time since you've tiptoed through some tulips, plants don't have legs. Jesus—the vine—doesn't ditch you. You're a branch. You need to stay connected to him.

Name something you're going to do to stick tight with Jesus this week.

DEEP THOT When you became a Christian, you established a tight vine-and-branch relationship with Jesus. But experiencing the coolness of closeness only happens when you *remain* in him. It's another way to look at that *responsive to God* thing.

ACT ON IT Talk with a mature Christian about how Jesus feels close and real to you—or not.

STICKY STUFF Hang tight to Jesus with John 15:5 in your head.

DIG ON Read some more of what Jesus had to say about fruit in Luke 6:43–46.

(25.) Best Friends Forever
(The greatness of God and good friends)

Toward the end of his time on earth, Jesus said he was heading back to his Father to build a heavenly place—not just for you, but for *us*, the people who trust in him (John 14:1–3). And the Bible book of Revelation shows you standing before God's throne with a multitude of others, shouting "Hallelujah! For our Lord God Almighty reigns. Let us rejoice and be glad and give him glory!" (Revelation 19:6–7). Remember? God's top-of-the-list goal for you is that you stick tight with him and with the people he's made. And that goal lasts forever.

BRAIN DRAIN How are you doing right now in hanging tight to God—and to his people?

FLASHBACK Think of this picture and twirl it around in your brain: *There's God . . . together with you and great friends . . . in a gargantuanly good place . . . both now and forever.* That's what God has planned for you. And that's what David wrote about in this next Bible Chunk.

BIBLE CHUNK Read Psalm 16:1–11

(1) Keep me safe, O God,
   for in you I take refuge.
(2) I said to the Lord, "You are my Lord;
   apart from you I have no good thing."
(3) As for the saints who are in the land,
   they are the glorious ones in whom is all my delight.

(4) The sorrows of those will increase
who run after other gods.
I will not pour out their libations of blood
or take up their names on my lips.
(5) Lord, you have assigned me my portion and my cup;
you have made my lot secure.
(6) The boundary lines have fallen for me in pleasant places;
surely I have a delightful inheritance.
(7) I will praise the Lord, who counsels me;
even at night my heart instructs me.
(8) I have set the Lord always before me.
Because he is at my right hand,
I will not be shaken.
(9) Therefore my heart is glad and my tongue rejoices;
my body also will rest secure,
(10) because you will not abandon me to the grave,
nor will you let your Holy One see decay.
(11) You have made known to me the path of life;
you will fill me with joy in your presence,
with eternal pleasures at your right hand.

STUFF TO KNOW Why does David trust God to take care of him (verse 1)?

David tells God that "apart from you I have no good thing." What's that mean (verse 2)?

SIDELIGHT David isn't saying that nothing is good in life except for God, but that everything good comes from God. In the New Testament, James says it like this: "Whatever is good and perfect comes to us from God above, who created all heaven's lights" (James 1:17 NLT). Still, David does think God himself is the ultimate great gift: "Whom have I in heaven but you? I desire you more than anything on earth" (Psalm 73:25 NLT).

God has sent another incredibly good gift David's way. What is it (verse 3)?

INSIGHT David calls people who follow the Lord "saints" and "glorious ones." He's radically happy about his friendship with those folks. But there's a night-and-day contrast between them and another group. . . .

Who is that second group? What are they up to (verse 4)?

INSIGHT If "libations [pouring out] of blood" sounds gory, it is. It likely refers to human sacrifices offered to fake gods (Isaiah 57:5–6).

Three metaphors here: "Portion and cup" is like what gets plopped on your plate, "lot" is where you live, and "inheritance" is short-hand for everything God gives you as his child. So what does David think of the life God is serving up (verses 5–6)?

Exactly how long will this good life last (verses 10–11)?

SIDELIGHT The New Testament applies that no-rot promise to Jesus (Acts 2:27). But that up-from-the-grave prediction of an eternity in paradise is about you too: Jesus said that because he lives, so will you (John 14:19).

BIG QUESTIONS What do you honestly think of God's plan for you to hang out with him and his friends for eternity?

What stands in the way of loving God and loving people being at the top of your to-do list? What are you going to do about it?

DEEP THOT To set the Lord always before you—and to put him at your right hand—means you make it your highest goal to live for him and obey his counsel, like his twin command to love him totally and love others as much as you love yourself. That sounds like the greatest life ever. What do you think?

ACT ON IT What's your plan to keep growing spiritually after you finish *Stick Tight*? Write it down—and share your commitment with a friend who will keep you on track.

STICKY STUFF Psalm 16:2–3 will help you keep in mind your Best Heavenly Friend—and your best human friends.

DIG ON Read Psalm 95 for more on how you and your friends can say great things about God—together.

Talk About It • 5

EMPATHIZE: What's going on in your life?
ENCOURAGE: How are you doing with Jesus?
EQUIP: What one truth will you take home today?

- When has a friend left you down and out? (Study 21)
- Who have you let down in the last few days? What can you do to straighten it out? (Study 21)
- Who do you turn to when your enemies jump you—and your friends dump you? (Study 22)
- How does God figure into your thinking when friends let you down? (Study 22)
- What's the first thing to ask God for when you feel friendless? (Study 22)
- Do you get nervous to be scrutinized by the all-seeing eye of God? Why or why not? (Study 23)
- How could it help you to be open with the God who knows you most—and likes you best? (Study 23)
- How do you stay connected to God—the best being in the universe you could ever be best friends with? (Study 24)
- Do you ever feel far from God? What makes you feel that way? What do you do about it? (Study 24)
- How are you doing right now in hanging tight to God—and to his people? (Study 25)
- What do you think of God's plan for you to hang out with him and his friends for eternity? (Study 25)
- What stands in the way of loving God and loving people being at the top of your to-do list? What are you going to do about it? (Study 25)

PUT YOUR LIFE
ON THE RIGHT PATH

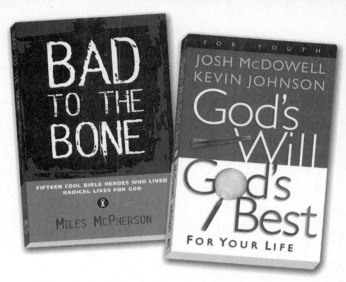

Understanding God's Will for Your Life

Happiness, a good career, good friends, and closeness with God are desires of everyone's heart. This book explains that God also desires to give these things to you—He even promises a specific plan for you to experience each of them. There's no catch, but there is a condition, a condition you can't afford to miss!

God's Will, God's Best
by Josh McDowell and Kevin Johnson

Life Lessons From Young Bible Heroes

Young Bible heroes like Daniel, Esther, and Josiah weren't afraid to go against the crowd. No matter what, they didn't back down from God's calling. They were committed to him all the way down to the bone, and God used them in supernatural ways. Want this for your life. Let this devotional rock you to the core!

Bad to the Bone by Miles McPherson

STICK TIGHT 5
Non-Christian friends
Mark 2:17 (NLT)

When Jesus heard this, he told them, "Healthy people don't need a doctor—sick people do. I have come to call sinners, not those who think they are already good enough."

STICK TIGHT 6
Being a servant
John 13:14–15

Now that I, your Lord and Teacher, have washed your feet, you also should wash one another's feet. I have set you an example that you should do as I have done for you.

STICK TIGHT 7
The qualities of a friend
Ephesians 5:1–2

Be imitators of God, therefore, as dearly loved children and live a life of love, just as Christ loved us and gave himself up for us as a fragrant offering and sacrifice to God.

STICK TIGHT 8
Comforting your friends
2 Corinthians 1:3–4 (NLT)

All praise to the God and Father of our Lord Jesus Christ. He is the source of every mercy and the God who comforts us. He comforts us in all our troubles so that we can comfort others.

STICK TIGHT 1
Love is a big deal
Matthew 22:37–39

Jesus replied: " 'Love the Lord your God with all your heart and with all your soul and with all your mind.' This is the first and greatest commandment. And the second is like it: 'Love your neighbor as yourself.' "

STICK TIGHT 2
Where love comes from
1 John 4:19

We love because he first loved us.

STICK TIGHT 3
Get godly friends
Hebrews 10:24–25 (NLT)

Think of ways to encourage one another to outbursts of love and good deeds. And let us not neglect our meeting together, as some people do, but encourage and warn each other. . . .

STICK TIGHT 4
God wants his love spread around the world
Matthew 28:19–20

Therefore go and make disciples of all nations, baptizing them in the name of the Father and of the Son and of the Holy Spirit, and teaching them to obey everything I have commanded you. And surely I am with you always, to the very end of the age.

STICK TIGHT 13
Christians are being remade

Titus 2:11–12 (NLT)

For the grace of God has been revealed, bringing salvation to all people. And we are instructed to turn from godless living and sinful pleasures. We should live in this evil world with self-control, right conduct, and devotion to God.

STICK TIGHT 9
You have gifts to offer your world

1 Corinthians 12:7 (NLT)

A spiritual gift is given to each of us as a means of helping the entire church.

STICK TIGHT 14
Being responsive to God

1 John 1:8–9 (NCV)

If we say we have no sin, we are fooling ourselves, and the truth is not in us. But if we confess our sins, he will forgive our sins, because we can trust God to do what is right. He will cleanse us from all the wrongs we have done.

STICK TIGHT 10
Standing up for what's right

Galatians 1:10 (NLT)

Obviously, I'm not trying to be a people pleaser! No, I am trying to please God. If I were still trying to please people, I would not be Christ's servant.

STICK TIGHT 15
You need Christian friends to survive

Hebrews 3:12–13

See to it, brothers, that none of you has a sinful, unbelieving heart that turns away from the living God. But encourage one another daily, as long as it is called Today, so that none of you may be hardened by sin's deceitfulness.

STICK TIGHT 11
How to find the best friends

Ephesians 2:4–5 (NCV)

But God's mercy is great, and he loved us very much. Though we were spiritually dead because of the things we did against God, he gave us new life with Christ. You have been saved by God's grace.

STICK TIGHT 16
Doing good to evildoers

Luke 23:34

Jesus said, "Father, forgive them, for they do not know what they are doing."

STICK TIGHT 12
God's definition of a Christian

Colossians 1:21–22 (NCV)

At one time you were separated from God. You were his enemies in your minds, and the evil things you did were against God. But now God has made you his friends again. He did this through Christ's death in the body so that he might bring you into God's presence as people who are holy, with no wrong, and with nothing of which God can judge you guilty.

Friends can let you down

Mark 14:72

Immediately the rooster crowed the second time. Then Peter remembered the word Jesus had spoken to him: "Before the rooster crows twice you will disown me three times." And he broke down and wept.

Conquering loneliness

1 Kings 19:18

"I have seven thousand people left in Israel who have never bowed down before Baal and whose mouths have never kissed his idol."

God is your most faithful friend

Psalm 27:4

One thing I ask of the Lord, this is what I seek: that I may dwell in the house of the Lord all the days of my life, to gaze upon the beauty of the Lord and to seek him in his temple.

God's top ten rules for relationships

Exodus 20:1–3

And God spoke all these words: "I am the Lord your God, who brought you out of Egypt, out of the land of slavery. You shall have no other gods before me."

God knows you inside and out

Psalm 139:1–2 (NCV)

Lord, you have examined me and know all about me. You know when I sit down and when I get up. You know my thoughts before I think them.

Four steps for getting along

Matthew 18:15 (NCV)

If your brother sins against you, go and show him his fault, just between the two of you. If he listens to you, you have won your brother over.

Sticking tight to Jesus

John 15:5 (NLT)

"Yes, I am the vine; you are the branches. Those who remain in me, and I in them, will produce much fruit. For apart from me you can do nothing."

Keeping on when evil wins

Malachi 4:2

But for you who revere my name, the sun of righteousness will rise with healing in its wings. And you will go out and leap like calves released from the stall.

God loves you at your ugliest

Romans 5:8

But God demonstrates his own love for us in this: While we were still sinners, Christ died for us.

The greatness of God and good friends

Psalm 16:2–3

I said to the Lord, "You are my Lord; apart from you I have no good thing." As for the saints who are in the land, they are the glorious ones in whom is all my delight.

God's love

John 3:16

"For God so loved the world that he gave his one and only Son, that whoever believes in him shall not perish but have eternal life."

Love for others

1 John 4:7–8

Dear friends, let us love one another, for love comes from God. Everyone who loves has been born of God and knows God. Whoever does not love does not know God, because God is love.

God's care

Psalm 46:1–2

God is our refuge and strength, an ever-present help in trouble. Therefore we will not fear, though the earth give way and the mountains fall into the heart of the sea.

God's unending love

Romans 8:38–39

For I am convinced that neither death nor life, neither angels nor demons, neither the present nor the future, nor any powers, neither height nor depth, nor anything else in all creation, will be able to separate us from the love of God that is in Christ Jesus our Lord.

Christian friends

2 Timothy 2:22 (NCV)

But run away from the evil young people like to do. Try hard to live right and to have faith, love, and peace, together with those who trust in the Lord from pure hearts.

God's unending love

Lamentations 3:22–23

Because of the Lord's great love we are not consumed, for his compassions never fail. They are new every morning; great is your faithfulness.